NOT ENOUGH

The Meaning and Measurement of Poverty in Canada

Report of the CCSD National Task Force on the
Definition and Measurement of Poverty in Canada

7976

ISBN 0-88810-346-8

Canadian Cataloguing in Publication Data
CCSD National Task Force on the Definition and Measurement of Poverty in Canada

   Not enough: the meaning and measurement of poverty in Canada

Bibliography: p.
ISBN 0-88810-346-8

1. Poor--Canada.   2. Poverty--Research--Canada
I. Canadian Council on Social Development
II. Title.

HV105.C47 1984   362.5'0971   C84-090111-9

The Canadian Council on Social Development
55 Parkdale Avenue
Post Office Box 3505, Station C
Ottawa, Ontario   K1Y 4G1

Printed and bound in Canada

6 5 4 3 2 1   84 85 86 87 88

Disponible en français sous le titre:

Trop peu: Définition et évaluation de
la pauvreté au Canada.

Foreword

The Board of Governors of the Canadian Council on Social Development, prior to the publication of its poverty line and <u>The Canadian Fact Book on Poverty 1983</u>, considered several challenges to the method whereby CCSD's poverty line was established and the assumptions upon which the method was based. The current definition used by the CCSD was developed in 1973 and consists of an income line based on one-half of the nation's average family income. The only adjustment made to this income line accounted for differences in family size. The Board consequently set up a task force, chaired by board members Alan Backley and Anne Usher to examine questions which challenged this method of defining poverty.

On behalf of the Council, I should like to thank all of those members of the task force who labored long over the many drafts of this report, the co-chairpersons who presided over its meetings and contributed so much to the production and refinement of the material, and to the task force staff, who guided the work and attended to the many details that made this project possible. Finally, a special thank you and note of appreciation to all the individuals and groups who took the time and interest to submit briefs and to make presentations at the public hearings.

Michael Clague
President
Canadian Council on Social Development

Contents

The Canadian Council on Social Development Task Force on the Definition and Measurement of Poverty in Canada

Co-Chairpersons

W. Alan Backley
Partner
Woods Gordon
CCSD Board Member
Ottawa, Ontario

Anne Usher
Community Worker
CCSD Board Member
Montréal, Québec

Task Force Members

Sam Blakely
Director of
   Social Services
City of Calgary
CCSD Board Member
Calgary, Alberta

Debbie Hughes
Community Liaison
National Anti-Poverty
   Organization (NAPO)
Ottawa, Ontario

André Joyal
Directeur
Module d'Economique
Université du Québec
Trois-Rivières, Québec

Jean Panet-Raymond
PLURA, Community Worker
Montréal, Québec

Penelope M. Rowe
Executive Director
Community Services
   Council
CCSD Board Member
St. John's, Nfld.

Joseph Ryant
Professor
School of Social Work
University of Manitoba
Winnipeg, Manitoba

Darlene Marzari
Businesswoman
CCSD Board Member
Vancouver, British Columbia

Jean Moore
Representative of Coalition of
  Provincial Organizations of
  the Handicapped (COPOH)
Kingston, Ontario

Eleanor Swainson
Credit Counsellor
Credit Counselling
  Service of Kingston
Kingston, Ontario

Peter Warrian
Assistant to the
  President
Ontario Public
Service Employees Union
Toronto, Ontario

Task Force Staff

David P. Ross
Coordinator

Lise Lutz
Secretary

Nancy Colborne Perkins
Researcher

Kathleen Warden
Support Staff

Tables and Figures

ANTOINE DÉSILETS, DES IMAGES PLUS

Introduction

Fundamental to any definition of a poverty line is its purpose. For the task force's purposes, the objective of being able to measure the number of poor households in Canada and to observe the trend of these numbers was paramount.

The task force examined the leading definitions of poverty, including that employed by the CCSD, to obtain some guidelines as to the standards of living or levels of well-being associated with various income levels. The next step was to determine what income level corresponded to an adequate basic living standard.

The task force discussed the two basic approaches for determining a basic income line -- the absolute and relative approaches. The absolute approach presumes that there is some fairly objective means for determining the absolute minimum a household requires for food, clothing and shelter. This minimum subsistence level is not much influenced by the standard of living that other households in society enjoy. On the other hand, the relative approach presumes that poverty can only be defined by looking at the standard of living enjoyed by the community in general. In this view, poverty can only be defined relative to prevailing community standards.

Having defined a basic income level, should adjustments to this living standard be made for differences in regional incomes and costs of living or for rural and urban residency? What distortions are caused in the poverty figures if wealth holdings are excluded from the income definition? Should adjustments be made for individual or household characteristics, for example, to accommodate the extra costs borne by persons with disabilities? Should adjustments be made to account for the availability (or lack) of subsidized public services?

Traditionally, poverty has been measured by establishing an income line and then making small adjustments for one or more of the factors mentioned above. This enables a measurement of the extent of poverty, that is, the number of households which fall below the line. The task force also examined two other dimensions of poverty that are often ignored, its "depth" and "length". Since many households have incomes far below the poverty line, should a measure of poverty describe how many and how far households fall below the line? And, since some households suffer low incomes for extended periods of time while others do so for only a short period, is it the length of time spent in poverty and the suffering of low incomes for long periods which produces the conditions of poverty?

In reaching its conclusions, the task force was guided by existing documents, statistics and the views of "experts". Additionally, a series of eight public meetings held across the country were designed to allow Canadians from all walks of life to share their views of what constituted poverty. Many participants were able to provide first-hand experiences of a life in poverty. A section of the report presents information gained from these public meetings as well as anecdotal and statistical descriptions of poverty in Canada in the 1980s.

The task force now presents its major findings on these questions and issues, and bases its recommendations on these findings.

Lessons from the Public Meetings

Public meetings were held in eight locations across Canada -- Vancouver, Calgary, Winnipeg, Toronto, Hamilton, Montréal, Trois-Rivières and St. John's -- which attracted approximately 400 participants. About 50 written briefs and comments were received during and after the meetings. Representative of the individuals and groups participating in the meetings were welfare rights groups, people on welfare, people with disabilities, government administrators, politicians, women's groups, human rights advocates, unemployed workers, social workers, church groups, academics and researchers.

Needless to say, these diverse groups saw different purposes being served by poverty lines, advocated different income support levels and approaches, and offered frank and contrasting views on the usefulness of the whole exercise. The meetings followed a general but not inflexible format; participants were given time to present a brief if they wished, following which task force members and other participants and observers asked questions and made comments. The atmosphere of the meetings was informal.

The task force learned that many of the participants did not want the Council to abandon its relative poverty approach, based on average Canadian income. Some believed it could be adjusted more precisely to account for regional income variation; but others saw regional adaptation as sanctioning lower regional incomes and therefore perpetuating the status quo. Other groups were not so committed to the idea of a national poverty line but wanted help in defining a line that would reflect local conditions and thus be more acceptable to the community.

The task force was reminded of the importance of accounting for free or subsidized services in determining the income poverty line. For instance, in B.C. many services are being cut back. Without these services, low-income people will need more money in order to cope. We learned that the disabled are constantly short of services and facilities, expecially those that foster independent living, such as an adequate transportation system, and aid in gaining access to employment opportunities.

The task force also heard that many so-called free services are not free. User charges for health care, the need for many rural users to travel great distances to avail themselves of "free" services, and the extra and mounting costs associated with "free" education, all act to restrict accessibility to these services. There were many instances where mothers on welfare were forced to keep their children at home on school days when a special event such as "hot-dog" or "sports" day was held because it required a fee, even though the fee may seem small to average-income families.

Women explained how their monthly welfare budgets were determined. On paper, everything appeared to work out fine: dollar allocations were made for a great variety of goods and services, adjustments were made for the number and ages of children, and certain special needs were recognized. But the harsh reality of these "paper" budgets was that shelter costs invariably ate up most of the budget. Consequently, allotted food money went to pay for the rent and allotted clothing money had to go towards food. In this way, mothers were forced to choose between providing one essential or another.

These women wondered why, if they were not going to be given enough money to live on or have a realistic assessment made of their needs, welfare administrations should bother constructing any budgets? Why not just give them the meagre amount and let them get on with it? It was often felt that failure to live on these budgets implied that the recipients were bad homemakers. There was a tacit assumption that welfare mothers should be "super-moms" capable of stretching inadequate sums of money a long way. In city after city, shelter cost emerged as the key variable in establishing adequate incomes.

What the task force learned about most of all was the existence of poverty itself. The low-income people attending the meetings did not wish to talk about the subtleties of poverty definition and measurement. They simply wanted to talk about the miserable and humiliating circumstances in which they found themselves. Some had been living this way for many years, but a few had only recently fallen into poverty, and some of these from a very adequate income level. These newly arrived poor now wondered why they had paid taxes for so many years and had contributed to what they thought was an adequate social security net. Now that they required assistance, they were appalled and distressed to find that the net was almost on the ground, that it was barely capable of allowing them to exist.

All of these people relying on social assistance were so far below anybody's poverty line that discussion of poverty was a futile exercise to them. Most wanted to know how they could get another $50 a month to put food in the fridge. Stories were told of fathers proudly absenting themselves from the dinner table because there was not enough food for even the children; of middle-aged women who live on $5 a day after rent is paid (an amount of money many of us pay for parking each day), out of which they had to pay for all their life's needs. When learning of the Statistics Canada poverty line, one woman exclaimed that it would represent "exotic living" for her family. These people were certainly not asking for the sky.

Their despair stems not just from a lack of money. There is also a feeling of being unwanted and of being shunned by mainstream society. Time and again, participants would come forward and begin their comments with, "I really shouldn't be here", "I know I'm going to make a fool of myself, but...", "I don't know why you would want to listen to me", "Why should I talk to you, you are not going to do anything about my situation anyway...". Some women openly expressed embarrassment at coming because they felt they "stood out" from other people. A few were surprised to find there were other people in like circumstances and harbouring the same feelings.

None of the meetings reached a consensus on how to define or measure poverty. But one thing was learned -- serious deprivation <u>does</u> exist in Canada. Whatever new definitions are developed are not going to define away the problem.

The task force believes that action, not further discussion, is now required.

The Purposes Served by Poverty Measures

One difficulty the task force had in arriving at a definition of poverty was the existence of the different purposes served by poverty lines.

At least four different purposes were isolated. The first centres on the desire to measure poverty. It is easy to discuss the wide range of social, psychological, political and economic factors that define poverty but difficult to quantify these factors in a way that is useful for measuring the numbers living in poverty. While it is important that poverty lines permit measurement, this objective also limits the definition.

A second purpose in defining poverty is to provide information and stimulus to those people administering programs, receiving assistance or advocating for change. As well, the way poverty is defined and measured can strongly affect the way the public views poverty and it can influence the desire of society to do something about it.

A third purpose of a poverty line is to establish a budget or expenditure level for those relying on public assistance or earning very low incomes. There is a natural temptation when confronted by households who are seeking public support to ask, What do these households need to survive? This leads immediately to budget-setting and to making judgements regarding the necessary items to be placed in the "market basket" of goods and services. Once the contents of the basket are chosen, it can be priced, and the cost becomes de facto a poverty line. In effect, welfare administrations across the country use poverty lines for the purpose of establishing subsistence levels of living.

A fourth purpose of defining poverty is to establish a goal or longer-term objective for income security policy. The original purpose of the CCSD income line, first developed in 1973, was to set a standard against which the alleviation of income disparity could be measured over time. This standard was based on an income of at least 50 per cent of the Canadian average, adjusted for family size. The issue here is not so much one of defining a survival budget but one of deprivation. The basis for the standard is the belief that households with less than one-half of average income are unable to participate fully in society -- either economically, socially or politically. The purpose behind this definition of poverty is to establish a measurable income goal against which social and income policy can be measured.

The Meaning and Measurement of Poverty

The need to measure poverty and to develop some objective social indicator that reflects the standard of certain Canadian households is paramount to the mandate of the task force. Hence, the measurement of poverty determines to a large extent how we define it. Unfortunately, objective indicators such as income levels, numbers, and the length of time spent living below a certain income level can never adequately define poverty. While a brief discussion of other dimensions of poverty is presented, there is in this report a preoccupation with defining poverty in a way that provides for its measurement but that admittedly is not comprehensive. A subsequent section on the "human face" of poverty attempts to overcome this shortcoming by portraying the multi-faceted nature of poverty.

Diagram·1
Schematic View of Well-Being

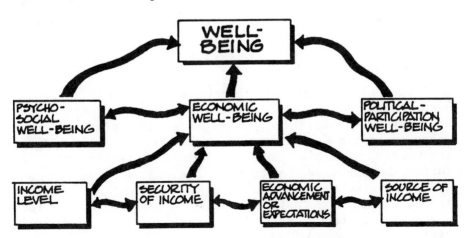

Three important dimensions of well-being are depicted in Diagram 1: economic, psycho-social and political-participation. Below a certain level of well-being, one can talk about the poverty of income, the poverty of spirit, and the poverty of power. One reason the task force did not pursue the psycho-social and political-participation dimensions is that criteria to define them are difficult to agree upon and to translate into objective terms. The other reason is that poverty is traditionally associated with a lack of income, which in turn is frequently associated with the poverty of spirit and of power. The three dimensions are highly inter-related. If a basic level of economic well-being is not achieved, the other aspects of well-being can seldom be fulfilled either. This is not to say that having a basic measure of economic well-being guarantees a happy and fulfilling life, but it is in most cases a necessary condition.

Within the category of economic well-being there are several other important factors in addition to level of income. One of these other factors is security of a given income level such as is provided through pensions, unemployment and sickness insurance, savings, wealth, and a steady job. Having a basic income above the poverty line is not an adequate guarantee for well-being if there is little security to that income. For low-income households, the psychological stress and the way it impairs economic well-being may be compared to living each day on a razor's edge: one is always wondering whether some sudden misfortune is going to reduce or take away the income.

Economic well-being almost certainly is influenced also by the source of income. For example, dependency on income transfers may be regarded as inferior to an earned income because of the stigma frequently surrounding certain forms of public assistance. An earned income gives a greater feeling of economic and social participation. Also, the capacity to earn an income usually provides greater choice of action, whereas state assistance is usually heavily circumscribed by regulation.

A survey conducted by "Single Mothers Against Poverty", a Hamilton group composed mostly of single mothers on social assistance, provided interesting results. Of 145 women who filled out a questionnaire that asked the family benefit recipients to "list the ways in which they have felt discriminated against", 73 per cent replied they were refused credit; 61 per cent replied they were judged as "welfare bums"; 51 per cent felt they were being judged on how they spent their money; 45 per cent perceived a "superior" attitude of the bank teller cashing their cheque; and 25 per cent responded that they were discriminated against when applying for a job.

Another aspect of economic well-being derives from the expectation of upward change and the potential for economic advancement. If the possibility for advancement is lacking, such as in many low-paying jobs, hopelessness is generated and detracts from economic well-being. College students invariably have low-incomes, but since upward change is almost assured, this temporary low-income state is seldom regarded as poverty.

While hard data are lacking, it is commonly understood that households with low incomes also generally have little security, receive the majority of their incomes from state assistance, and have little prospect of economic advancement. People in other income groups may also occasionally suffer from one or more of these circumstances, but not to the same degree or with the same persistence as low-income persons. What these different aspects of income poverty convey is that people with persistently low-incomes do not simply live scaled-down versions of the lifestyle of middle-income people; they are in fact required to lead markedly different lives. Poverty is a "package" of economic conditions of which low income is only one -- security, source and prospects of income also strongly condition this package and the lifestyle that results from it.

NATIONAL FILM BOARD — PHOTOTHÈQUE

The Human Face of Poverty

The task force feels strongly that statistics or income lines cannot adequately describe the plight of those living on low incomes. The following stories are thus presented to illustrate a variety of life situations across Canada.

From **Vancouver**, a woman wrote down her feelings for the task force:

"You asked: What does poverty mean to me?

Well, to me poverty means not being able to buy food that is nutritional, instead of spaghetti and potatoes with the occasional two pounds of hamburg. I don't go to the food bank because I don't want to take food from someone who may need it more than me.

Not having that all-important job to go to.

Not being able to buy even the cheapest clothes to put on my back.

Doing the laundry in the bath tub because I can't afford to go to the laundromat.

Making sure that I make my phone calls before I leave home. I can't afford to give B.C. Tel. any of my precious quarters.

Not being able to buy someone you know the odd cup of coffee.

Losing people you called friends because you're now a bum and not of the fit and proper working class.

Having absolutely no sense of security and worrying about what will happen if you get sick or die at home. In my case, no one would know for a week or more.

Wanting to sell some of your personal effects and knowing that if you do, they will simply deduct it off your next cheque.

Feeling like dirt, now that I'm broke.

Having the government always cut back on the poor and not on themselves. The rent, phone, hydro, food, etc., goes up continually, but my spending capital in fact goes down with each raise in expense.

Dreading every time you have to go to the welfare office, walking slow before you get there, then making a dash for the door, hoping no one sees your face as you go in to beg again".

And from **Alberta**:

Ms. B. is a single-parent woman, 34 years of age, with two school-age children (8 and 10). Ms. B. is physically handicapped and requires prescription drugs. As of July 1, 1983, this family's shelter allowance was $505 per month. Their three-bedroom apartment in the inner city, including utilities and one parking spot, is $700 a month. The casework supervisor has authorized an additional $150 a month in excess of the shelter allowance since the oldest child is doing well in the neighborhood elementary school and the apartment owners allow children. Their food and tobacco allowance as of July 1, 1983, is $361 a month. A single-parent family in Calgary with two school age children would spend approximately $350 per month in order to eat nutritiously but simply, that is, no baked goods or frozen pre-cooked foods. The family's clothing and household allowance is $129 a month. Since a "no-frills" pair of denim slacks for boys is approximately $15, the two boys wear hand-me-downs. Ms. B. does some sewing, but the machine is worn and there is no money left at the end of the month for incidentals, such as having the sewing machine fixed. An application to the Burns Memorial Fund for Children has been submitted in order to send the boys to summer camp. In summary, after necessities, that is, food, clothing and shelter, there is no discretionary income.

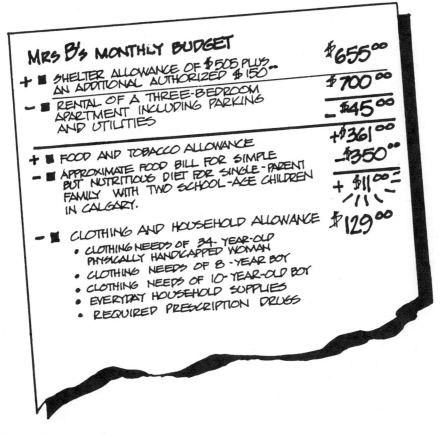

MRS B's MONTHLY BUDGET

+ ■ SHELTER ALLOWANCE OF $505 PLUS AN ADDITIONAL AUTHORIZED $150

$655⁰⁰

− ■ RENTAL OF A THREE-BEDROOM APARTMENT INCLUDING PARKING AND UTILITIES

$700⁰⁰

−$45⁰⁰

+ ■ FOOD AND TOBACCO ALLOWANCE

+$361⁰⁰

− ■ APPROXIMATE FOOD BILL FOR SIMPLE BUT NUTRITIOUS DIET FOR SINGLE-PARENT FAMILY WITH TWO SCHOOL-AGE CHILDREN IN CALGARY.

−$350⁰⁰

+ $11⁰⁰

− ■ CLOTHING AND HOUSEHOLD ALLOWANCE

$129⁰⁰

  • CLOTHING NEEDS OF 34-YEAR-OLD PHYSICALLY HANDICAPPED WOMAN
  • CLOTHING NEEDS OF 8-YEAR BOY
  • CLOTHING NEEDS OF 10-YEAR-OLD BOY
  • EVERYDAY HOUSEHOLD SUPPLIES
  • REQUIRED PRESCRIPTION DRUGS

Another case in **Calgary** involves a male quadraplegic, 21 years old. He was injured in an accident in 1979, employed at the time of the accident as a truck and auto body worker.

Before cutbacks were announced, he was independent, living in a one-bedroom apartment with stores, a bank, a barber, a restaurant, a post office, medical offices, etc., in the same building and was receiving paramed in-home assistance. He was taking correspondence courses with the possibility of post-secondary education in the future, and enjoyed a good social life. He was independent with Handi Bus, was coping well with shopping, and was able to obtain needed special protein food. In general he was happy and content with his lifestyle.

Cutbacks in social services made it necessary for him to move into shared accommodation with three adults and two children in a rented house in a rural area of Calgary. There is no guarantee that he can stay there longer than one year. The cost of moving and changes are his personal responsibility.

An ambulance will now be required for any medical attention whereas before, a VON or paramedic could make a house call. Paramed service required for dressing assistance is not available from the rural health unit and although Paramedics are willing to come, they cannot do so without charging. His social life is now restricted. He is unable to pack and move on his own. Dependency on friends caused him anxiety. He is having difficulty getting special diet food, and shopping is very difficult. Handi Bus does not go beyond the city limits so transportation difficulties discourage future attendance at educational institutions.

This man receives public assistance of $744 a month. After paying for paramed services and rent, he has $190 left for basic needs, diet requirements and Handi Bus transportation.

— — — —

The husband of a married couple with a 6-year-old daughter was laid off in June 1982. The wife is also unemployed. They received a social assistance subsidy of $127 until UIC benefits expired in June 1983. Social assistance was cut off the following month because neither adult had found a job. Both filed an average of 35 job searches a month as instructed by their case worker. When cut off, they were unable to pay the rent, and so moved into a travel trailer parked in a relative's yard and sold all their assets except a van and the trailer. They reapplied for assistance two months later and were given an appeal date for later in the month, along with one emergency food voucher. A breakdown in family relations saw this couple and their child roaming the city in the trailer for nearly a week pending their appeal. They were given one night's emergency accommodation in a motel. The appeal reinstated benefits for two months only.

— — — —

16

And from **Toronto**, several histories drawn from the files of a social agency:

- A young mother subsisted on water and cookies from our nursery for the last week of the month before her welfare cheque arrived. Her rent was $224 a month out of a welfare cheque of $404.
- An eight-month-old infant consumed two 8-ounce bottles of milk within 30 minutes of arriving at the nursery because the mother had no food at home. When taken to the doctor, the child was found to have an ear infection, but he had not cried with pain because of extreme lethargy. The mother's rent was $200 a month out of a welfare allowance of $369.
- A mother with a year-old child, unable to afford better accommodation, keeps the light burning in their bedroom all night because it keeps away most of the cockroaches from the sleeping child. Out of an income of $403 she pays $269 rent.
- A pregnant teen depends on Scott Mission for food during the last week of every month - it is the only way to subsist after paying monthly rent of $225 out of her $305 welfare allowance.
- An 18-year-old woman with a child had the courage to leave her abusive husband but has been living in a hostel for 3½ months, unable to find employment or accommodation.

- - - -

From **rural and smaller town Ontario:**

"Between the age of 8 months (when I contracted polio) and 18 years, I spent at least one session a year in the hospital. My parents could not afford to pay the doctors all at once so monthly doctor bills were the rule until I began to work at 18 and finished them off myself.

My braces and special shoes were paid for by the Ontario Society for Crippled Children. Poppa worked two jobs most of the time to cover the medications and extras I needed.

To keep my secretarial job, I worked longer hours and much harder to balance out the fact that I couldn't walk long distances at the block-long building, nor could I hurry. About one-third of my pay went for medicines and special shoes because I was now too old to be covered by existing assistance programs.

After I married, my pregnancies (three) were much more complicated, so they cost more than normal. As my health deteriorated, a tubal ligation was suggested and agreed to. Dental care was non-existent because medical care had to be looked after first.

At 40 I was put back into a full leg brace for which we had to pay $350.

I imagine this sounds like a soap opera and that some will say we are better for the struggle; however, life could have been much more enjoyable if organizations in the past were more aware of the needs of the handicapped."

- - - -

Jim and Gloria are 29 and 28 years old and have two daughters aged 7 and 2. Jim was formerly employed as a skilled worker in an industrial plant. He enjoyed modestly good wages, with which he was able to buy a small house.

A year ago, Jim was permanently laid off, along with many other workers from the same industry. Shortly after, Jim and Gloria lost their home and managed to find a cheap apartment in a housing development run by a religious charity. Eventually Jim obtained employment pumping gas at a local filling station. Since his wages were less than his UIC entitlement, he was subsidized until his benefits ran out. Now he and his family must live solely on his wages of $4 an hour, which results in a gross income of $704 a month (net of $620) plus a family allowance of $58 for a total of $678 a month.

This is how Jim and Gloria spend their money:

rent	$260
telephone	10
cable	7
laundry	20
life insurance	19
food	320
church	20
transportation	20
	$676

They have $2 left to cover clothes, prescriptions, dental care, entertainment, etc. They neither drink nor smoke, and their social life revolves around the church. They still can't make it.

Jim is very bitter. He comments: "The government says it is involved with job creation and that Canadians should accept any kind of work -- well I have, and look where it's gotten me -- I can hardly feed my family. I'd never go on welfare, but I can sure understand the people who do."

- - - -

From **Montreal**; an admission clerk, 29 years old with 17 years of schooling:

"You feel the pressure and the stress all the time. But you tell yourself that you're not out on the street, that you have enough to eat, that your kids are healthy except that you find you're getting poorer, that you're not getting ahead. I'm very disappointed. You don't even dare to dream. I had dreams three years ago but don't anymore."

- - - -

A young couple, 22 and 25 years old have a combined income of $15,100 a year. Formerly a shipping clerk, he is now unemployed. She works in a shoe factory but lost her seniority when she was unemployed two years ago. They were living with her parents to try to save money for their own home, but conflicts developed, and all their savings were depleted when the husband became unemployed. They have cut back on most purchases of clothing, food, cigarettes and gas and must stay at home for vacations.

– – – –

A couple with 3 children, the husband, 47, works as a guard; his wife, 41, works as a beneficiary clerk in a hospital. Their combined income is $26,515 a year. Their salaries are "frozen" because of government cutbacks with no advancement possible, yet they cannot risk job changes without losing 9 and 10 years of accumulated seniority. They must organize their work schedules so that they avoid babysitting costs for their 5-year-old child. The husband had a second job, but ill health will no longer permit this. Their budget must be tightly controlled for there is no safety margin and they are finding it increasingly difficult to keep up with inflation. They have quit smoking and cut down on the use of the car to save money.

– – – –

And from **Newfoundland**:

An elderly couple in their 70s were living in a shed with no running water. It was heated by a woodstove for which wood had to be hauled. The gentleman was blind. Both of them were receiving old age pensions and had enough money to live on, but they were not physically or mentally capable of looking after themselves. They had no bedclothes and no dishes, and they were being exploited by some of their neighbours. It took over a year of advocacy on the part of our association [Provincial Human Rights] to convince the social services people that this couple should be put in a situation where they could receive proper homemaker services and be allowed to live at a level of dignity.

– – – –

The high cost of drugs and medical aid is something that our Provincial Human Rights Association is very concerned about. We are finding that people are neglecting their health needs because they cannot afford to pay for medical and dental services or their drug requirements.

- - - -

Another case involves a single-parent female who is presently forced to live in the bedroom of a friend's house. She has two children, one of whom is in a wheelchair with cerebral palsy to such a severe degree that the child cannot move. Yet the woman cannot get a house from provincial housing authorities because she is not a priority on the waiting list. They do not say what their priorities are, but poverty or loss of dignity cannot possibly be one of them.

- - - -

Yesterday we [Newfoundland Status of Women Council] spoke with a 22-year-old single-parent mother of two, aged 5 and 3. Alice was pregnant and married at 15. She knew nothing about birth control and had quit school at Grade 10.

Eighteen months of marriage left her a victim of domestic violence with two babies and a drastic change in her financial status. Alice, however, has managed to complete high school through night courses and one year of clerical training at Trades & Technology ... without any financial support from the father of her children. As a mechanic he made good money but refused to pay maintenance and the courts can't find him.

Over the past five years, Alice has combined social assistance with cleaning jobs, babysitting jobs and office work. She is presently maintaining two part-time clerical positions and taking home $832 monthly. She would like not to have to wash clothes by hand, but she can't afford a washer or the laundromat. She would like to buy new clothing as opposed to second-hand. She would like to afford more nutritious food for her children, for example, milk rather than coloured Freshie. But her status as a single parent denies her and her two children access to a decent standard of living.

- - - -

The majority of the preceding case histories involve women. This is not accidental. Poverty in Canada today does indeed have the face of a woman, and feminization is poverty's outstanding feature. Poverty also deeply affects persons with disabilities, as the case histories demonstrate. However, because income and employment statistics on the disabled are not systematically collected, it is not possible to identify and document the extent of their poverty.

To set these case histories in the perspective of over-all poverty, Table 1 illustrates the likelihood of people with different characteristics falling into poverty. For example, single-parent mothers have a 43 per cent chance, lowly educated family heads a 19 per cent chance, and women over the age of 65 and living alone face a 62 per cent chance of being poor.

The information in Table 2, rather than illustrating the likelihood of being poor, shows the distribution of all poor people by certain characteristics. The information shows that 30 per cent of all poor families are headed by women and that 52 per cent of all poor families have the family head in the labour force. Among unattached individuals, those over 65 years of age constitute 44 per cent of the poor (the majority being elderly women).

Four Measures of Poverty

Estimates of income lines derived from four different approaches follow:
- the implied poverty lines of provincial welfare administrations
- the Toronto Social Planning Council budget guidelines
- the CCSD poverty lines
- Statistics Canada's low income cut-offs.

1983 POVERTY LINES

	Family of One	Family of Four
Social Assistance (Average of long-term provincial rates):	$3,956	$9,860
Social Planning Council of Metropolitan Toronto (estimated budgetary requirements);	$10,145	$20,455
Canadian Council on Social Development	$8,625	$20,125
Statistics Canada's Low Income Cut-offs: (rural-urban)	$7,052-$9,538	$14,268-$19,397

7976

25

SOCIAL ASSISTANCE RATES

The social assistance rates paid by the different provinces vary considerably (see Figures 1 and 2). It may not be entirely correct to refer to social assistance levels as poverty lines; certainly the provinces do not. But effectively, and after the fact, they do represent what the different provinces consider to be the minimum amount below which people will not be allowed to fall. It is supposed to be a basic needs level.

This belief is further strengthened by the fact that all administrations do establish budgets for social assistance recipients, based on minimum subsistence market baskets they develop themselves. These budgets pay scant attention to needs other than food, shelter, and clothing, except in special cases usually involving health problems. Participants in the public meetings gave us graphic evidence of the unrealistic nature of some of these budgets.

Social assistance rates are based on a market basket chosen almost without regard to what other people in the community have in their baskets. The approach tries to estimate an absolute level, unrelated to community standards, that is considered necessary to feed, shelter and clothe members of a household at the absolute minimum level. At all the public hearings, the task force was told by people who are experiencing life on social assistance that administrations succeed in finding the lowest minimum. There can be no doubt that, for most, life on social assistance is unhealthy, nerve-wracking and humiliating.

In a brief submitted in Winnipeg by the Manitoba Anti-Poverty Organization, which provides assistance to low-income persons, the following extract describes the shortcoming of subsistence budget approaches:

"During the one-year period August 1982 to June 1983, approximately 800 files were opened for assistance with welfare problems. One of the major concerns expressed by welfare people was "trying to make ends meet" on the welfare budget. Most people

Figure 1

Annual Social Assistance Benefits and Other Transfers, by Province, for Single Parent Family with Child, 1983

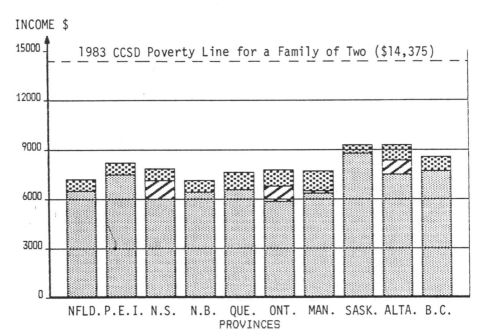

INCOME $

1983 CCSD Poverty Line for a Family of Two ($14,375)

PROVINCES

NFLD. P.E.I. N.S. N.B. QUE. ONT. MAN. SASK. ALTA. B.C.

▦ : SHORT-TERM SOCIAL ASSISTANCE RATE

▨ : LONG-TERM SOCIAL ASSISTANCE RATE, AVAILABLE ONLY IN N.S., ONT., MAN., and ALTA.

▦ : ANNUAL INCOMES AS A RESULT OF ADDING IN FEDERAL CHILD-RELATED TRANSFERS AND PROVINCIAL TAX CREDITS, WHERE APPLICABLE, TO THE PROVINCIAL SOCIAL ASSISTANCE RATES

NOTE: SHORT- AND LONG-TERM RATES ARE DEFINED BY RELEVANT PROVINCIAL ACTS/REGULATIONS.

Source: Social Planning Council of Metropolitan Toronto, Infopac 1983, Vol. 2, No. 4

Figure 2

**Annual Social Assistance Benefits and Other Transfers, by Province, for a
2-Parent Family with 2 Children, 1983**

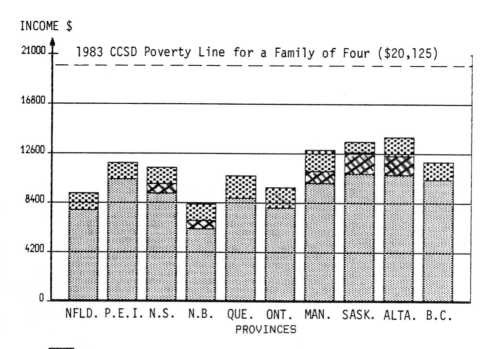

INCOME $

1983 CCSD Poverty Line for a Family of Four ($20,125)

PROVINCES

: SHORT-TERM SOCIAL ASSISTANCE RATE

: LONG-TERM SOCIAL ASSISTANCE RATE, AVAILABLE ONLY
IN N.S., N.B., MAN., SASK., and ALTA.

: ANNUAL INCOMES AS A RESULT OF ADDING IN FEDERAL
CHILD-RELATED TRANSFERS AND PROVINCIAL TAX CREDITS,
WHERE APPLICABLE, TO THE PROVINCIAL SOCIAL
ASSISTANCE RATES

NOTE: SHORT- AND LONG-TERM RATES ARE DEFINED BY RELEVANT
PROVINCIAL ACTS/REGULATIONS.

Source: Social Planning Council of Metropolitan Toronto,
Infopac 1983, Vol. 2, No. 4

complained that the allowances received from welfare for basic necessities -- food, clothing, household supplies and housing -- were just too low.

As an example, one of our clients, a female head of the household with three children -- a six-year-old boy and two girls, 13 and 14 -- receives the following budget from welfare each month:

	Food	Clothing	Personal Needs	Household Supplies
1 Adult	90.50	23.60	27.90	8.10
14-year-old Girl	101.40	30.00	NIL	2.70
13-year-old Girl	101.40	30.00	NIL	2.70
6-year-old Boy	68.00	20.00	NIL	2.70
	$361.30	$103.60	$27.90	$16.20

Employed adults may add $16.70 for clothing.

The total food budget of $361.30 a month for a family of four is not adequate, according to the much acclaimed Canada Food Guide. The cost of purchasing the basic food staples outlined in the Guide, such as meat, fish, poultry, cheese, juice and milk for a family of this size far exceeds the food allowance provided by welfare. The monthly food allowance budget of $90.50 for one adult is particularly meagre."

TORONTO SOCIAL PLANNING COUNCIL GUIDELINES

The Toronto Social Planning Council (SPC) also uses an approach based on a market basket, but as the figures show, the income result is considerably different. The fact that two market basket approaches can lead to much different results clearly shows that one approach is based on a bare subsistence concept and the other on a relative poverty concept.

The Toronto Social Planning Council develops its budget with the help of experts and advisory panels drawn from the community, and since 1949 the broadly based basket that has been developed partially reflects what other members of the community have in their baskets. One could call it a relative market basket approach (see Appendix A for a broad listing of items).

Living on the Toronto SPC budget cannot be considered "fancy living" by any means. It could be more appropriately described as "scraping by", as compared to social assistance short-term "minimum subsistence". It is the judgement of the Toronto SPC that the budget they describe is exceeded by 70 to 75 per cent of all Toronto households; that is, it is an extremely modest budget. The Toronto SPC also develops special budgets for single parents and the elderly, recognizing the special needs of these groups.

The Toronto SPC approach has a drawback in that it is specific to Toronto, and from a national perspective this may present a problem, although it has been adjusted for use in at least three other cities -- Vancouver, Hamilton and Winnipeg. The Social Planning and Research Unit of the Vancouver and Lower Mainland United Way has published sets of low-income basic budgets for 1982.

CCSD POVERTY LINE

Since 1973 the Canadian Council on Social Development has employed the relative income approach, then it set its poverty line at 50 per cent of average Canadian family income.

The CCSD line is constructed quite simply, based on the prevailing value of the average Canadian family income as estimated by Statistics Canada. The income figure represents pretax income. In 1983 the average Canadian income figure was considered to represent the income of a family of three (the average Canadian family size). The poverty line for a family of three is calculated as 50 per cent of the average income figure. Adjustments are then made for different-sized families on the basis of family income units (a family income unit is considered to be the annual amount necessary to sustain a dependent). Family-size adjustments are then scaled -- a family of one is granted three income units; a family of two has five units; a family of four has seven units, and so on.

STATISTICS CANADA LOW INCOME CUT-OFFS

The closest Canada comes to an "official" national definition of poverty, that is, the definition adhered to by the federal government, is that developed by Statistics Canada. This method is best described as a relative expenditure approach. Whereas the Council bases its line on average income in the community, Statistics Canada bases its line on average expenditure in the community.

The Statistics Canada lines are based on surveys of household expenditures, the latest conducted for 1978 when it was estimated that the average Canadian family spent 38.5 per cent of its income on the basic necessities of food, clothing and shelter. Statistics Canada then made the judgement that any household required to spend more than 58.5 per cent of its income on these basics would have so little discretionary income remaining that it would be living in "straitened circumstances". Since these surveys also reveal that the fraction of income spend on basics declines as income rises, Statistics Canada is able to locate the low-income level at which a typical household spends 58.5 per cent or more of its income on basics. This income level then becomes the "low income cut-off" after adjustments have been made for different family sizes and urban/rural residency. The line is then adjusted annually by the full amount of change in the consumer price index.

SUMMARY

The value of either of the market basket or budget approaches is that they translate into terms or images highly recognizable and understandable to the public. They are also based on local costs. Consequently, basket approaches are capable of fulfilling several of the purposes of poverty lines. The Toronto SPC, but certainly not the social assistance approach, also provides a reasonable objective for income policy.

The other two general approaches to defining poverty, adopted respectively by the CCSD and Statistics Canada are national in scope and are based on the incomes and expenditures of all Canadians. The CCSD approach is based solely on the country's income distribution. This relative income comparison defines poverty, or deprivation, in terms of whether a household has considerably less income than others. This method views low income as entirely relative to other incomes in the community. The relative income approach springs more from the principle of equity than it does from a concern simply to provide for the basic necessities of life.

The shortcomings of national lines are manifold. First, they lack imagery. As statistical lines they do little to convey the hardship of living on the stated amounts as our earlier case histories show. Pure dollar figures have little impact. Second, local groups do not always see these lines as applying to their communities for purposes of developing budgets; the lines are seen more as "national averages". Third, there is a certain amount of arbitrariness embodied in their construction. Why does the Council choose 50 per cent of average income? Why does Statistics Canada include only food, clothing and shelter in its basket and then choose a 20 per cent mark-up on the average expenditure on these three items?

The strengths of the lines are also manifold. First, they are simple to calculate and understand. Second, they provide unvarying standards that lead to fairly easy measurement of the low-income population. Third, they establish national, as opposed to local or regional goals or objectives that we can pursue as a nation.

The Adjustment Factors

The Council's Fact Book on Poverty, 1983 presented several factors for which a national income standard could conceivably be adjusted. Consideration of the appropriateness and/or feasibility of making adjustments (beyond family size) for different factors was a major preoccupation of the task force. It considered the following factors: geographic income differences; regional cost of living differences; rural/urban expenditure differences; extra costs associated with disability; family wealth; and subsidized public services. The following sections summarize what the task force learned about these factors.

GEOGRAPHIC INCOME DIFFERENCES

Family incomes vary by province and by rural-urban setting. Figure 3 illustrates provincial income differences for 1971 and 1981. As a percentage of average national family income, the provincial shares ranged from 76.1 per cent in P.E.I. to 113.5 per cent in Alberta. During the period 1971-81, the Atlantic provinces improved their shares considerably with the biggest improvements being registered by Newfoundland and P.E.I. In fact, with the major exception of Alberta, which moved from below to above the national figure and to a minor extent, Québec, which edged slightly downwards, all provinces moved towards the national average.

Incomes also varied within the provinces depending on whether the household was located in an urban or rural area. As the following data show, the rural-urban income differences are substantial, and

Figure 3

Average Provincial Family Income, As a Percentage of National Average, 1971 and 1981

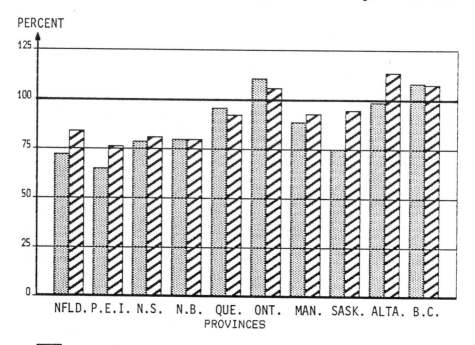

PERCENT

: 1971 AVERAGE PROVINCIAL INCOME

: 1981 AVERAGE PROVINCIAL INCOME

Source: Statistics Canada, <u>Income distributions by size</u>
<u>in Canada</u>, 1971 and 1981

this has prompted Statistics Canada, in developing its poverty lines, to adjust to rural-urban income differences.

Size of Area of Residence	Family Income (1981)
Urban areas with population exceeding 100,000	$33,001
Urban areas with population between 30,000-99,999	$28,543
Small urban areas under 30,000	$27,536
Rural areas	$26,190

For comparison with our largest cities, 1981 average family income was as follows: Toronto, $35,616; Montréal, $30,383; Vancouver, $35,344; Edmonton, $37,275; Winnipeg, $29,384; and Halifax, $28,791. While the task force acknowledges geographical differences in incomes, it does not necessarily follow, as Statistics Canada presumes, that the cost of living varies in a corresponding fashion. The cost of an adequate market basket would seem to be the key issue to explore or on which to base variations in poverty lines. To accept and adjust poverty lines downward for lower incomes in the Atlantic provinces and in rural areas seems only to institutionalize these low incomes. The key question is the extent to which the cost of living varies across the country.

COST OF LIVING DIFFERENCES IN URBAN CENTRES

What is the purchasing power of a given level of income across Canada? Is it markedly cheaper to live in certain regions or provinces? Do low incomes and low costs go hand in hand? These are the basic questions relative to poverty-line adjustments.

Surprisingly, there is little comprehensive data on a representative market basket for all provinces. We have consequently resorted to several sources that can be used to give an impression, these sources being Statistics Canada consumer price indexes for a limited market basket and for cities only; a Conference Board

Table 3

Inter-city Indexes of Retail Price Differentials, as of September 1983, for Selected Groups of Consumer Goods and Services (combined city average = 100)

COMPONENTS	ST. JOHN'S NFLD.	CHARLOTTETOWN PEI.	HALIFAX N.S.	ST. JOHN N.B.	MONTREAL QUE.	OTTAWA ONT.	TORONTO ONT.	WINNIPEG MAN.	REGINA SASK.	EDMONTON ALTA.	VANCOUVER B.C.
Food purchased from stores	107	98	94	101	100	94	101	95	101	101	105
Household operations, furnishings and equipment	105	101	105	107	98	100	102	97	97	96	104
Transportation	101	96	95	95	107	98	100	92	91	92	100
Health & Personal Care	102	95	104	100	98	100	102	97	94	106	104
Recreation, Reading & Education	106	104	108	106	98	101	102	97	98	98	101
Tobacco & Alcohol	129	102	99	108	101	100	101	101	102	93	103
	650	595	605	617	602	593	608	579	583	586	617

Source: Statistics Canada, Consumer prices and price indexes, Oct-Dec. 1983

of Canada market basket survey; and a special survey conducted for the task force, with items selected from a representative low-income market basket but primarily for urban areas.

Table 3 presents the results of a Statistics Canada pricing survey for 11 cities (clothing and shelter are not included in the survey). Taking 100 as the index for the weighted price of all cities, we see, for example, that with respect to purchased food, prices ranged from a high of 107 in St. John's to 94 in Halifax and Ottawa. The weightiest item in this survey, transportation, varied from a high of 107 in Montréal to 91 in Regina.

The only specific impression gained from these data is that St. John's would seem to have higher overall costs than the prairie cities. But the general impression gained is how close all the indexes are to the average value of 100, with the exception of low transportation costs on the prairies, and the high cost of alcohol and tobacco in St. John's. The cost data are marked by more similarities than differences.

The major shortcoming of this Statistics Canada survey is that the items cover only about 60 per cent of a family's market basket (as noted, the most conspicuous absences are clothing and shelter). To overcome this, the task force conducted, with the generous assistance of volunteers, a market basket price survey of a more representative sample of items. Partial results of this survey are contained in Table 4, with more detail provided in Appendix B and the questionnaire that was utilized in Appendix C.

Again, as with the Statistics Canada data, the overall impression is of similarity rather than difference across the cities. While specific items may cost more in some cities than others, the difference tends to be cancelled out by the price differential on other items. The task force does not deny that differences exist, but we are struck by the small degree of price variation, and by the fact that there is no substantial and systematic variation in urban

Table 4

Task Force Budget Summary National Cost of Living Comparison, February/March 1984

ITEM	REGIONAL COSTS $									
	ST. JOHN'S NFLD.	CHARLOTTETOWN PEI	GLACE BAY N.S.	ST. JOHN N.B.	MONTREAL QUE.	KINGSTON ONT.	OTTAWA ONT.	SASKATOON SASK.	CALGARY ALTA.	VANCOUVER B.C.
1. FOOD:	45.16	40.70	38.73	39.07	46.39	46.36	39.19	40.75	42.29	41.83
2. HOUSEHOLD SUPPLIES:	10.83	10.14	6.10	10.05	11.50	12.37	10.12	11.54	10.40	11.18
3. PERSONAL CARE SUPPLIES:	6.37	5.77	4.70	5.47	5.62	5.90	4.23	6.28	4.68	5.58
4. HOME FURNISHINGS:	1066.73	1045.42	879.91	1383.70	1183.91	949.68	1184.87	1144.67	1146.66	1140.90
5. ALCOHOL & TOBACCO:	46.81	32.70	29.39	36.27	26.69	30.59	31.25	31.24	29.09	31.89
6. READING, RECREATION, EDUCATION:	135.90	160.73	148.10	168.85	162.90	129.15	153.48	150.80	121.00	161.43
7. MEDICINE CHEST SUPPLIES:	9.64	11.35	7.67	10.10	13.52	7.88	8.97	10.34	10.96	8.74
8. CLOTHING:	370.49	379.73	382.84	363.24	388.91	378.87	361.95	371.39	385.33	379.99
9. HOUSING:	789.00	710.00	662.50	576.00	564.35	657.00	735.00	625.00	874.00	917.00
10. TRANSPORTATION:	44.46	*	*	*	46.74	55.99	67.79	*	*	78.86

* Public transit is not available in all locations. See detailed cost of living comparison in Appendix B.

All items priced were exclusive of sales tax except the Alcohol & Tobacco items.

An attempt to assess a cost of living comparison for Winnipeg was unsuccessful.

living costs to which a national income standard could
feasibly adjust.

Finally, the results of a survey conducted by the
Conference Board of Canada tend to reach the same
conclusion. In contrast to the task force survey, the
Conference Board survey assumed a rather higher
lifestyle market basket associated with an income level
of $45,000. The results summarized in Figure 4 show a
marked similarity among the cost-of-living indexes --
being almost identical in St. John's, Montréal, Toronto
and Vancouver.

Figure 4
Index of Total Family Expenses, 1983, (index, Montreal = 100)

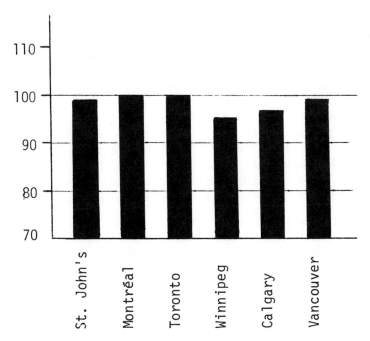

Source: Adapted from The Conference Board
of Canada

The difference in total living costs (including income taxes) between the lowest cost city, Winnipeg ($41,643), and the highest cost, Montréal ($43,655), is only $2,012, or less than 5 per cent.

RURAL-URBAN EXPENDITURE DIFFERENCES

All of the above three sources of cost of living information deal with urban areas, and unfortunately, comprehensive information on the cost of living in rural areas can only be gained impressionistically from Statistics Canada expenditure data, last gathered for the year 1978.

Income data presented earlier showed that rural incomes are 78 per cent of family incomes in the three largest metropolitan areas and that Statistics Canada, in making allowances for its low income lines allows a 73% difference between rural low-income lines and those for the largest cities. From these figures, the conclusion could be drawn that life is considerably cheaper in rural areas. Certainly there is a popular view that rural dwellers are more self-sufficient and have lower costs. But expenditure data for 1978 show that in total dollar terms, rural dwellers spend 88 per cent as much as urban dwellers, even though their incomes are much less than that in percentage terms. On the basis of this finding, one is drawn either to the conclusion that country dwellers simply spend more or else that they are required to pay higher prices for those items they do purchase. A detailed look at their expenditures for 1978 supports the latter conclusion.

The information in Table 5 shows that even with considerably lower incomes, rural dwellers (must) spend markedly more dollars than urban dwellers on transportation, shelter repairs, water, fuel and electricity, household appliances, children's clothing, and prescribed medicine. Few of these items could be considered discretionary or non-essential. Items that

Table 5

Summary of Family Expenditure, by Size of Area of Residence in Canada, 1978

EXPENDITURE ITEM	AVERAGE DOLLAR EXPENDITURE		RURAL EXPENDITURES AS A % OF URBAN
	URBAN (Pop. 500,000+)	RURAL (Farm/Non-Farm)	
1. Food	3408.9	3010.5	88.3
2. Shelter	3424.3	2414.3	70.5
- Repairs & Maintenance	261.2	324.9	124.4
- Water, Fuel & Electricity	536.1	794.8	148.0
3. Household Operations	814.7	727.2	89.3
4. Household Furnishings & Equipment	868.3	837.7	96.5
- Furniture	298.4	234.0	78.4
- Appliances	168.1	191.2	113.7
5. Clothing	1308.3	1162.8	84.2
- Women 14 yrs+	678.2	508.7	75.0
- Girls 4-13 yrs	52.8	71.3	135.0
- Men 14 yrs+	493.3	416.3	84.0
- Boys 4-13 yrs	53.8	65.1	121.0
- Children (under 4 yrs)	29.9	38.6	129.1
6. Personal Care	342.7	254.6	74.3
7. Medicine & Health Care	400.2	353.7	88.4
- Dental Care	119.0	82.2	69.1
- Physician	10.6	5.4	50.9
- Prescribed Medicine	45.7	57.1	124.9
8. Tobacco & Alcohol	654.3	530.7	81.1
9. Transportation	2356.9	2689.0	114.1
10. Recreation, Reading & Education	1244.5	971.8	78.1
11. Miscellaneous Expenditures	449.1	490.1	109.1
12. Personal Taxes, Security & Gifts	5174.5	3331.3	64.3
- Personal Taxes	3818.5	2314.6	60.6
- Life Insurance Premiums	190.5	149.9	78.7
- Retirement and Pension Fund Payments	500.7	313.8	62.7
- Gifts and Contributions	465.6	417.3	89.6
13. Savings	986.4	247.4	25.1

Source: Statistics Canada, Family expenditure in Canada, 1978, vol.3.

some may consider somewhat more discretionary are those that rural dwellers stint on: furniture, women's clothing, personal care, dental and medical care, tobacco and alcohol, and recreation. Thus these expenditure patterns would strongly suggest that rural dwellers have considerable difficulty in maintaining essential expenditures with their lower incomes.

The information suggests that in addition to less spending on more discretionary items, four factors permit rural dwellers to spend a greater proportion of their incomes on the necessities of life: lower taxes; less expended on security items such as life insurance and retirement funds; less savings, and lower shelter costs. In interpreting the above expenditure data it should be noted that rural family size exceeds urban family size by about one-half a person. Consequently, some expenditures would be expected to be slightly higher.

The impression gained from this brief examination is that the rural cost of living, as represented by expenditure data, is not cheaper -- except for shelter (see Appendix D for more detail). Even the lower shelter expenses may not reflect cheaper dwelling costs as much as they do lower quality and smaller homes. With the knowledge already gained concerning the lack of significant differences in cost of living across the provinces in urban areas, and in the absence of convincing data to the contrary, there is little reason and no statistical basis for adjusting a national line to place of residence. For low- to moderate-income families, it is not substantially and systematically cheaper to buy the basic items that constitute an adequate market basket in rural areas or in certain provinces. The notion that basic living is less costly in rural areas would appear to be just that -- a notion.

However, while remaining unconvinced of substantial and systematic geographical differences in the cost of living, the task force does believe that some groups in society face substantially higher costs than most

Canadians just in order to function at basic economic and social levels. One such group consists of persons with disabilities.

Unfortunately, while there is a common understanding that persons with disabilities do systematically face higher costs, there is little comprehensive or reliable information on the extra costs associated with disability. One of the problems is that there are many forms of disability, each with its own particular needs. Other factors, such as the availability of specialized services and whether or not family or friends are available to assist, will greatly alter financial needs.

Figure 5 illustrates the extra amount that is granted to single persons with disabilities. The average for all provinces is $134 a month. The amounts provided do not necessarily reflect the true additional costs faced by these persons but simply that provincial authorities already recognize substantially higher costs. In some provinces, the provision of specialized services is used as a means for giving assistance to persons with disabilities.

To stress the need to recognize the extra costs associated with disability, two illustrative case histories are presented. The first concerns a woman confined to a wheelchair and requiring a special diet:

Being in a wheelchair, J.M. is unable to buy life insurance and take part in most pension plans; she therefore invested in income property while still working and able to meet mortgage payments and have maintenance done. Since she is unable to do any odd chores, maintenance bills are high unless friends volunteer their time. Fifteen years of property management have taught J.M. that tenants often try to take advantage of a landlady, especially one in a wheelchair. While the income property is a valuable asset, it could not be liquidated without completely disrupting her lifestyle. In her own home J.M. has rewired, put in new plumbing, and had other major

Figure 5

Total Financial Assistance Available to an Unattached Individual with Disability, including Annual Social Assistance Benefits and Provincial Tax Credits, by Province, 1983

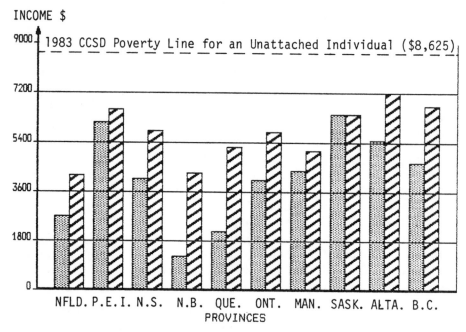

INCOME $

1983 CCSD Poverty Line for an Unattached Individual ($8,625)

PROVINCES

NFLD. P.E.I. N.S. N.B. QUE. ONT. MAN. SASK. ALTA. B.C.

▦ : UNATTACHED INDIVIDUAL

▨ : UNATTACHED INDIVIDUAL WITH DISABILITY

Source: Adapted from the Social Planning Council of Metropolitan Toronto, Infopac 1983, Vol. 2, No. 4

renovations done to accommodate her disability. Because she was employed, the Ontario Ministry of Community and Social Services bought her a wheelchair lift and door-unlocking mechanism, but because of her salary at the time ($18,500), no other financial help was available. The Department of Community and Social Services also bought her a motorized wheelchair and has paid for several repairs on it, and as well has paid for 10 hours a week of homemaking. If much of her attendant care was not volunteered by family and friends, this would cost a monthly minimum of $40.

Other expenses include a Blue Cross premium ($26 monthly), food (being diabetic, J.M. requires a well-balanced diet), and clothing (when working J.M. requires professional attire and because of her wheelchair, there are additional cleaning bills as well as the increased vulnerability caused by frequent laundry procedures). Some of her clothing, like pantyhose, is subject to more strenuous wear, and thus requires more frequent replacement. J.M. wears orthopedic shoes, which cost a minimum of $115 a pair. While Blue Cross does pay 80 per cent of prescription drugs and non-motorized wheelchairs, the residual 20 per cent fee is often considerable, and the insurance does not cover extra requirements like wheelchair cushions ($50-$300, depending on the kind prescribed). Since it is time-consuming and much more of an effort for her to write, her telephone bills are higher. J.M. maintains an electric typewriter ($124 annually) although IBM donated the typewriter itself (this is not common to person with disabilities). J.M. does not own a car, but travels by bus for the handicapped and gets rides with family and friends. If the bus for the handicapped is not available, taxi-travel is the only alternative.

J.M. finds her recreation mainly through entertaining family and friends in her home. Almost no wine or alcohol is used, and no cigarettes. Much of the food is donated. She enjoys live theatre, but financial constraints make it a rare treat. Outside entertainment also incurs transportation costs where in many cases the able-bodied could have walked.

J.M. finds herself in the position of having to accept financial hand-outs despite extensive scrimping, and an Honours BA.

– – – –

The second history has been provided by a social agency:

George is 40 years old. Born with congenital deformities, he has spent his entire life in a wheelchair and will continue to do so. He has some use of his hands and arms and can live in moderate independence as long as he has the assistance of a homemaker several days a week. Because he requires a ground floor easy-access apartment, he is housed in a senior citizens' apartment complex, in which and from which he can move about with relative convenience. Prior to this arrangement, he was a resident in a nursing home for the elderly.

George has a Grade 12 education plus additional interest courses. He reads widely and speaks optimistically if not realistically about finding a job and working his way off public assistance. He has no patience with those on assistance who are not actually physically disabled, is politically conservative, and is dedicated to the principle that anyone can find a job if he looks hard enough. He is cheerful about his condition, his future and even his meagre income.

George is on a disability pension of $364 a month provided by the provincial social services department.

rent	$ 66	(geared to income)
food	150	
telephone	25	(because of a hearing
transportation	15	disability, an extra
drug store items	5	gadget is needed for
haircut	4	the phone, which increases
newspapers, magazines	10	the rate)
cable TV	7	
membership fee	7	
entertainment	15	
church	36	
cigarettes	12	
laundry	12	
	$364	

If George has to purchase an item of clothing, he runs behind on other budgeted items. He owes about $1,000, comprised entirely of debts in the $10 to $20 range; to a number of friends, and is frustrated and ashamed at his inability to pay it back.

MISCONCEPTIONS OF FAMILY WEALTH

It is sometimes stated that low income cut-offs, or poverty lines, are not sufficient for measuring poverty because they do not account for wealth. How relevant is this concern?

From the point of view of statistics gathering, "wealth" is defined as net worth (assets minus debts). The data show that any such wealth holdings among low-income households are primarily in the form of real assets such as houses and vehicles. Overall, the poorest 20 per cent of households in Canada in 1977 (most recent year for which comprehensive data are available) held only 9 per cent of the country's wealth and their position deteriorated between 1970 and 1977. On the other hand, the top 20 per cent of Canada's households held 44.3 per cent of the nation's wealth in 1977.

Concentrating on net worth (wealth) in Table 6, low-income homeowners (under $7,000 income group) had on average net worth of less than $50,000 (in 1977), and for non-homeowners it was less than $5,000. Although it is not shown in this table, it is known from expenditure surveys that this home ownership is heavily concentrated among the aged and among rural dwellers. For the middle-income group ($10,000-$20,000), the net worth of homeowners is only about $5,000 more than that of low-income homeowners. But the non-homeowner counterparts in this middle-income group have greater wealth. By comparison, the highest income group, those with an income of $25,000 and over, had wealth holdings of up to $215,001 for homeowners and $45,711 for non-homeowners.

Table 6
Household Net Worth

NET WORTH (WEALTH) OF FAMILIES AND UNATTACHED INDIVIDUALS, BY TENURE AND BY INCOME GROUPS, SPRING 1977

Average Net Worth	Under $3000	$3000 - 4999	$5000 - 6999	$7000 - 9999	1976 Income Groups $10000 - 14999	$15000 - 19999	$20000 - 24999	$25000 - 34999	Over $35000
All Families and Unattached Individuals	16,656	23,338	24,077	31,001	33,511	40,612	46,567	67,939	205,859
Home Owners	47,278	52,395	49,265	61,676	55,891	54,800	55,327	75,739	215,001
Non-Home Owners	2,182	4,592	4,606	6,219	7,864	10,213	15,017	45,711	

Source: Adapted from Statistics Canada, Income, assets, and indebtedness of families in Canada, 1971

Although it is not presented in the table, the average amount of liquid assets (such as money, stocks and bonds) held by low-income households was only worth about $3,700, and this figure does not take into account any debt obligations. Middle-income households held an average amount of liquid assets equal to $6,000. Households with incomes exceeding $35,000 held over $24,000 worth of liquid assets. But it should also be pointed out that with respect even to the moderate $3,700 worth of liquid assets held by low-income households, 50 per cent of these had holdings of less than $700. Consequently, because of a concentration of holdings among a relatively few households in this low-income group, the average figure quoted above of $3,700 is quite misleading. The majority of low-income households in fact have virtually no liquid assets, and the lack of wealth is yet another aspect of their lowly lifestyle. Moreover, in most cases, any wealth they do hold is in the form of their house or equity interest in their farms or businesses (tractors, trucks, tools). To transform these assets into cash would detract considerably from their already lowly and fragile lifestyles. To put it differently, low-income households do not hold their small amounts of wealth in easily converted stocks and bonds and other securities like wealthier households do.

In conclusion, there is little validity to the claim that income measures of poverty significantly overstate the number of low-income households because poor people have substantial wealth holdings. As a result, the task force does not think it is a serious shortcoming to continue to ignore making any wealth adjustments in a national poverty line.

SUBSIDIZED PUBLIC SERVICES

One of the objections to a national income line is that it does not accurately reflect standards of living because of variations in the availability of subsidized services across the country. While the task force feels this to be an important issue, it is not an issue that can be systematically adjusted for at the regional or provincial level, for two reasons.

First, it is hard to ascertain any systematic differences in the basic provision of health, education and social services across the country. There are certainly more similarities in basic provision than there are differences. This is primarily due to a common understanding among Canadians that these services are public and that they receive basic funding from the federal government. Consequently most services have been required to meet certain basic standards. And it is basic standards we are concerned with here.

Second, while there are no substantial differences in the basic provision of social services across the provinces, there are undoubtedly differences with respect to access to such services by individual households. But this varies within provinces, counties, municipalities and even within cities. It is well known and the task force heard frequently that factors such as distance, family responsibilities, disability or minimum user fees can effectively render subsidized services inaccessible.

To come back to the adjustment problem, how can a poverty line that is to be useful beyond any individual household take into account that subsidized medical and education services exist in certain localities but that there may be many who cannot gain access to them or who have to pay a heavy price to receive them?

Thus the task force came to the conclusion that adjustment for free or subsidized services at regional or provincial levels is not required because marked differences do not exist on any systematic or substantial basis. Differences do exist across certain households, and it would technically be possible but in practice very difficult to ask householders to estimate the dollar value of subsidized services received by them and to add this amount to their incomes. Thus some households who may be judged "poor" on the basis of money income alone, may cross over the poverty line when the value of "in kind" social services is added on, and conversely, households that had to pay large sums to avail themselves of services might drop below the line.

The task force has not adopted this type of approach because it is not practical and because it would make little difference to the number being classified as poor each year.

The Dimensions of Poverty: Extent, Depth, and Length

Current statistical measures of economic poverty concentrate only on the extent of poverty. For example, each year both Statistics Canada's low income cut-offs and the CCSD's poverty line contain estimates of how many families live below their respective lines. The resultant number, taken as a percentage of all Canadian families then becomes the poverty rate or the extent of poverty in Canada. The task force is convinced that this single measure of the state of poverty in Canada is inadequate and possibly misleading. Both for the purpose of expressing the hardship of poverty and for developing appropriate policy responses, the depth and length of poverty are also required information. Fortunately, it is relatively easy to prepare indicators to express the depth of poverty, and the task force develops some of these below. Unfortunately, it is not possible to advance the length dimension very far because of the lack of data.

THE DEPTH OF POVERTY

The task force has frequently encountered the belief that poor people live <u>at</u> the poverty line. When the Council releases it poverty line estimates each year, people are heard to say, "Well, that seems like enough money to live on. Why are poor people complaining?" In fact, very few of the poor live at or even near the line. And the hardship of poverty grows with the depth.

Figures 6, 7 and 8 show for different family sizes that compared to the CCSD poverty line in 1981, many families and individuals are far below the line, some a bit below, some around it, and most well above it. Appendices E, F and G present income distribution data for different family sizes that reinforce the concern that many people are far below the existing poverty lines.

One way of transforming the illustrative approach employed in Figures 6 to 8 into an objective indicator to represent the depth of poverty is to calculate the average payment per unit that would be necessary to raise all families and unattached individuals to the CCSD poverty line. Having made this calculation for the years 1971 and 1981, in 1981 dollar terms the "average depth" of poor households was $3,450 in 1971 and $4,000 in 1981. Over the decade, the average depth has grown.

To further elaborate the depth dimension, Appendices H and I present data on a regional basis showing the share of a region's population falling below the CCSD line. The share falling below one-half of the poverty line is also shown to emphasize the depth dimension. This information shows, for example, that over 20 per cent of the families on the prairies fall below the CCSD poverty line, and 5 per cent fall below one-half of the poverty line.

THE POVERTY GAP

One way of transforming the extent (rate) and depth measures into an objective indicator is by using a measure known as the poverty gap. The poverty gap is simply the product of the depth and extent, which measures the total (not average) amount of money required to bring all low-income households up to the poverty line, that is, to close the poverty gap.

Calculations for 1971 and 1981 are contained in Table 7 and show that in terms of 1981 dollars, the gap has increased from $5.8 to $9.3 billion over this 10 year period. It is also evident that the growing gap is caused both by a larger number of families being

Figure 6
The Depth of Poverty — Distribution of Income, All Families, 1981

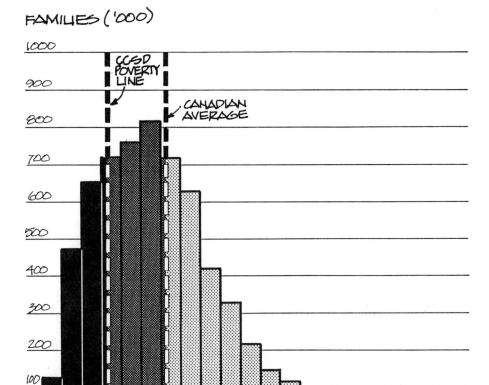

FAMILIES ('000)

SOURCE: STATISTICS CANADA, <u>INCOME DISTRIBUTIONS BY SIZE IN CANADA,</u> 1981 AND UNPUBLISHED DATA FROM THE SURVEY OF CONSUMER FINANCES, 1982

Figure 7

The Depth of Poverty — Distribution of Income, Unattached Individuals, 1981

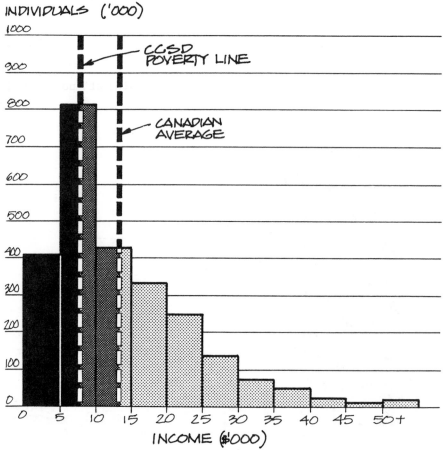

INDIVIDUALS ('000)

CCSD POVERTY LINE

CANADIAN AVERAGE

INCOME ($000)

SOURCE: STATISTICS CANADA, INCOME DISTRIBUTIONS BY SIZE IN CANADA, 1981 AND UNPUBLISHED DATA FROM THE SURVEY OF CONSUMER FINANCES, 1982

Figure 8

The Depth of Poverty — Distribution of Income, Family Size Three, 1981

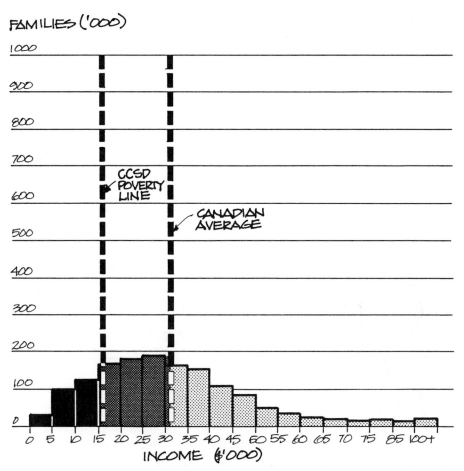

SOURCE: STATISTICS CANADA, INCOME DISTRIBUTIONS BY SIZE IN CANADA, 1981 AND UNPUBLISHED DATA FROM THE SURVEY OF CONSUMER FINANCES, 1982

below the poverty line, and by them being further below the line.

In terms of the country's capacity to finance a closing of the gap, this has remained relatively unchanged, requiring nearly 3 per cent of gross national product or 4 per cent of total household income in 1981. Thus, while the poverty gap has increased, the ability to eliminate or close it has not changed.

Table 7
The Poverty Gap

	1971	1981
Household poverty rate	24.7%	25.7%
Number of households below CCSD poverty line	1,685,000	2,307,000
Gap between actual incomes and poverty line (1981 dollars)	$ 5.8 billion	$ 9.3 billion
Gap as percentage of GNP	2.6%	2.8%
Gap as percentage of total household income	4.1%	4.0%

THE LENGTH OF POVERTY

How long do specific individuals or households endure their low-income status? Throughout our lifetime is it roughly the same 20 per cent of households who are poor (thus possibly generating a poverty trap for succeeding generations), or is there a constant changeover of households? Curiously enough, although this dimension of poverty is at least as, if not more, important than the extent and depth dimensions, there is virtually no information for Canada beyond anecdotes and conjecture. Fortunately, the initial results of a longitudinal study involving around 5,000 families over a 10-year period in the U.S. are now being made public (the results may not reflect Canadian experience).

Briefly, the results show that

- many of the commonly held stereotypes of "typical welfare cases" and "the poor" really apply to the exception rather than the norm;

- of families who had ever drawn welfare over the 10- year period, fewer than 1 in 12 (8 per cent) had relied heavily on welfare for more than seven years, and almost one-half received welfare for no more than one or two years over the 10-year period;

- one in every four Americans lived in a family that received some welfare income over the 10-year period.

These are only a few of the more general observations resulting from the study. What they show is that less than 2 per cent of the U.S. population had a long-term dependency (more than seven years) on welfare. There is a considerable degree of changeover in the poverty population with people entering and then escaping it. This is attested to by the high number (25 per cent) of individuals who had lived in families receiving some welfare payments.

The only data available for Canada covers income changes between two years, and although the results must be treated with extreme caution, they do suggest some turnover in the poverty population over a one-year period. Also, the families being examined here are "working poor" and not those dependent on welfare assistance.

Table 8 presents the results of this study, which traced changes in the income status of "working poor" households between 1971 and 1973. Of the 1972 "very low" income group, 48 per cent remained in that status in 1973, while 24 per cent and 27 per cent moved up to "supplementation" and "higher" income levels respectively. Thus about three-quarters of the very low income group remained as wage-earning poor.

Of the 1972 supplementation (moderately low income) group, 43 per cent remained at that income level, 12 per cent fell into the very low income group, and 45 per cent advanced to the higher income group. Thus slightly more than half of the supplementation group remained as wage-earning poor. Of the 1972 higher income group, 96 per cent retained that income status in 1973 with only 4 per cent falling into the wage-earning poor category.

Table 8
1973 Destination of 1972 Wage-earning Poor Families

1972 Income Group	1973 Income Group			
	Wage-Earning Poor			
	Very low	Supplementation	Higher	Total
Very low income	48.1	24.5	27.3	100
Supplementation	11.9	42.7	45.4	100
Higher income	1.0	2.9	96.2	100

During this two-year period then, there is some evidence of an escape from poverty, but the depth of poverty seems important, with the very low income group showing the greatest likelihood of remaining in poverty. Although the poorest of the wage-earning poor have only one chance in four of advancing to a non-poor status, the moderately low wage-earning poor have almost a fifty-fifty chance of moving out of their poverty status for at least one year. Data limitations prevent any further speculation with regard to these families beyond 1973.

Do all families that advance into the higher level group remain there permanently, or do they fall back into poverty either temporarily or permanently? The data on the 1972 higher income group initially tend to suggest that they stay there, only 3.4 per cent falling into poverty. But because the higher income group represents such a relatively large share of Canadian families (around 80 per cent), 4 per cent of this group constitutes a very large fraction of the 1973 low-income families. After adjusting for this in 1973, for example, 27 per cent of the supplementation families consisted of formerly higher income families. Consequently, the possibility of slipping back into poverty appears greater when adjustments are made for the relative sizes of the groups.

These data, however, almost certainly overstate the potential to escape poverty for all low-income households. The above data pertain only to the working poor and not to those on longer-term social assistance. The elderly, persons with disabilities, the chronically ill, and many single-parent mothers have less likelihood of escaping poverty or do so only after a long spell.

The task force is unfortunately unable to conclude its examination of the length of poverty dimension with any useful adjustments to present poverty measures. The length dimension is, however, an important variable in understanding the hardship associated with low income as well as the appropriate policy response. In fact it is quite likely that the length a household suffers low income marks the difference between "low income" and "poverty". While "having a low income" and "being poor" are often used interchangeably (although not by Statistics Canada), the difference, when it exists, can likely be attributed primarily to length. If a household records a low income for a period of a few months or even a year (depending on past savings and future prospects) it will not necessarily consider itself poor in the sense of having a life marked by extreme economic hardship and lack of social amenities. It is when the low income persists that the resulting enforced way of life may be described by the word poverty.

Obviously, it is highly significant both for policy and advocacy purposes whether the households classed as having low incomes are only temporarily poor or have been or will be poor for many years, or forever. Few members of the public are going to be concerned about poverty if there is a belief that the turnover is high. And from a policy standpoint, short-term poverty primarily requires a focus on income maintenance, whereas long-term poverty requires a focus on education, social services, employment policy and manpower services. Statistical surveys in Canada give only a "snap-shot" of the incomes of those covered by the survey. What we need are long-run surveys like the one being conducted in the United States. How households fare in the years immediately preceeding or following the survey year is not recorded in Canada. As a result, the task force is able to convey little more than an impression of the importance of this dimension of poverty.

Findings of the Task Force

1. Basic poverty and deprivation still exist in Canada. Many households are living unhealthy, hazardous and humiliating lives because they lack income. This may be a reflection of the inadequacy of poverty measures in that the present approaches, by being too abstract or difficult to understand, do not convey or convince other Canadians of the hardship suffered by people on low incomes.

2. In the public hearings and as expressed by the official poverty data, poverty is becoming overwhelmingly associated with women -- younger single-parent mothers and the elderly widowed. In 1981 Statistics Canada estimated that of all poor families, 30 per cent were headed by single-parent mothers and that the likelihood or incidence of poverty was 43 out of every 100 for this type of family.

   Of all poor unattached individuals that year, 44 per cent were over 65 years of age, and the National Council of Welfare estimated that 57 per cent of the elderly were female. For every 100 elderly women, 62 were likely to be poor.

3. Although the elderly in general have shown continued improvement over the years, their low income position is now being taken over by the young and by persons with disabilities. Young individuals or family heads and persons with disabilities are finding it increasingly difficult to receive permanent and well-paying employment. Over one-half of those defined as "poor" today are known as the working poor. These are people who rely for their major source of income on earnings

from the labour market. In recent years this type of poor person has become more prominent among the low-income population. Unfortunately, official income data does not specify persons with disabilities, however from the evidence presented at our public meetings, it is apparent that disability and low-income status are often related.

4. One of the main purposes of a national poverty line is to set a goal towards which social and income policies can be measured. It is a standard by which progress can be judged, a standard to ensure that Canadians across the country have access to at least a basic and similar minimum standard of living. This basic standard should not be developed in terms of subsistence living. Rather, it should be developed so that persons and households are able to feel they are a part of their surrounding society's activities and able to participate fully in them without stigma and without "standing out".

5. The task force was unable to find, either in its public meetings across the country or in the available data, any reason to accept a national poverty standard based on geographic income variations. Because of this, the task force has not adopted adjustments for differences since this could be interpreted as condoning the present unequal geographic distribution of income. One of the main purposes of a national poverty line is to set a national standard for reducing, not maintaining, wide income disparities.

6. The task force found that a representative basket of goods and services in total, costs nearly the same wherever a person resides in Canada. In this respect, the commonly held belief that rural living is markedly cheaper than urban living is a myth. Rural incomes are less, and this leads to a reduced standard of living, but to turn this around and then claim that it is cheaper to live in the country has no real basis in fact. All the

evidence suggests that country dwellers skimp considerably on less important basics, are able to attain little economic security, and likely endure lower quality housing in order to satisfy more urgent needs. The provision of public services in rural areas is often absent or insufficient, and where services are available, residents frequently must travel longer distances and at greater cost than their urban counterparts. The cost of a package of basic goods and services does not vary significantly between urban and rural areas. Where there are favourable cost differences in particular items, they are offset by unfavourable differences in other items.

7. In looking at adjustment factors beyond geographical variations in incomes or cost of living, the task force concluded that other variations were primarily of a personal nature. To begin to adjust the poverty standard to individual circumstances would require perhaps nine million poverty lines -- one for each Canadian household. It would also require making a large number of questionable value judgements. For example, would an efficient, well-organized household be required to accept a lower income (poverty line) than a wasteful, less careful household? Or if because of circumstance or preference a household has more specialized and expensive needs, would we adjust the income line upward to accommodate this? In arriving at a national standard, we have concluded that "on average" this amount of income provides a basic adequate standard of living. The possibility of adjusting to individual circumstance is rejected.

8. The one exception to making adjustments is for persons with disabilities who do "on average" face higher costs wherever they live. A given income corresponds to a lower standard of living where a household contains one or more disabled persons. Consequently, the national standard could not be expected to apply to persons with disabilities.

Since, however, the extra costs associated with disability vary considerably with the nature of the disability and with the availability of public services geared to their special needs, the amount to be added to the national standard would have to be calculated after consultation with a wide variety of organizations of persons with disabilities. Unfortunately, the task force was unable to gather enough useful data on this subject matter to conclude with precise cost adjustments.

9. From evidence heard at the public meetings, the task force was strongly reminded of actual or threatened cutbacks in universal social services such as health care and education. Many cases of retrenchment in providing access to other services such as day care, legal aid and other family services were identified. The imposition of health care user fees, the charging for school textbooks, the increasing number of special event days at schools, escalating college and university tuition, and the curtailment of services in some areas means that income takes on added importance when additional fees are applied to formerly free or subsidized services.

10. In arriving at its decision to maintain a national poverty standard at 50 per cent of national average income, the task force was influenced considerably by the results of the detailed and community-based market basket budget procedure worked out by the Toronto Social Planning Council and described in this report. The Social Planning Council's budget calculation falls within a few hundred dollars of 50 per cent of national average family income.

The Canadian Council on Social Development poverty line, based on national average income, and the Toronto Social Planning Council approach, based on detailed budgets, complement each other. The 50 per cent standard adds a national dimension and simplicity in calculation. The Toronto SPC approach fleshes out the 50 per cent standard by translating it into everyday expenditure patterns that are easily understood. It is possible to visualize the type of life a 50 per cent standard provides. Examination of the budget allows one to see that while it is adequate it is also very frugal.

11. The task force has found that the measurement of only the extent of poverty, or its rate, is an inadequate measure of poverty. In addition to the extent, there are two other dimensions: depth and length. Consequently, the task force has presented additional data on the depth of poverty, or more precisely, how far household incomes fall below the poverty line. The conclusion is reached that since 1971, the depth has increased. Unfortunately, because Canada maintains no statistics on the length of time that people suffer low incomes, it is not possible to incorporate this important dimension in the national measure. The limited data that are available, however, suggest that the low-income population is not stable; that is, there is some turnover in its composition.

12. At the time of writing, in the Spring of 1984, the task force is relying on 1981 data. For policy purposes, a two- to three-year lag in information is serious, for it means policy is formulated in reaction to a situation described statistically three years ago. This kind of lag would not be tolerated in the collecting and reporting of data on leading economic indicators. Moreover, this lag is not owing to technical impediments but rather to a low priority attached to this information.

13. The task force has also found other shortcomings in official income data. For example, natives living on reserves are excluded from the annual income surveys. Because it is common knowledge that most native reserves suffer from low incomes,

the official poverty statistics understate the extent of low incomes in Canada.

14. Statistics Canada also presents no regular data on persons with disabilities. This has made the task force's examination of the nature and extent of the relationship between disability and low income extremely difficult and incomplete.

Recommendations

On the basis of its broad findings, the task force makes the following recommendations concerning the meaning and measurement of poverty:

1. A national income standard can and should be used for defining and measuring poverty. This standard would vary only for family size and for disability.

2. The income standard would be based on 50 per cent of national average family income, which in 1984 is estimated to be $36,226 before taxes, and would vary for family size according to the following schedule:

CCSD 1984 POVERTY LINES

Family Size	Poverty Line
1	$9,056
2	$15,094
3	$18,113
4	$21,131
5	$24,150
6	$27,169

These incomes will provide in all areas of the country an adequate budget as developed by the Toronto Social Planning Council, which used the help of community based panels and expert evaluators.

3. Adjustments to the national poverty standard to account for the extra costs associated with disabilities need to be worked out with the assistance of organizations of persons with disabilities.

4. The depth of poverty and a dollar measure of the "poverty gap" should be published annually with the other data on poverty. Evidence suggests that although the extent of poverty has stabilized somewhat in the past decade, the depth has increased.

5. For policy purposes, the problem of poverty can best be comprehended by using the "poverty gap" measure. This measure illustrates the amount of money required to bring all low-income households up to the 50 per cent national standard. In 1981 the poverty gap amounted to $9.3 billion, or 2.8 per cent of the gross national product.

6. Since the length of poverty is an important dimension of poverty and because no data is regularly or comprehensively collected on this dimension, the government should commission a longitudinal study to repair this deficiency. A similar study nearing completion in the United States is contributing greatly to an understanding of the problems of poverty. This study has extended over 15 years.

7. Because of the "feminization" of poverty, increased attention should be paid to the special problems of women.

8. Although the task force feels that there is little difference in the cost of purchasing a basic standard of living in rural or urban areas, there is need for a more systematic examination. The task force suggests that the wide discrepancies in the low-income lines used by Statistics Canada are more the result of income than cost differences. Statistics Canada should collect and publish cost-of-living comparisons specifically for rural areas based on a range of basic items of similar quality.

9. The task force also recommends to the Government of Canada that at least three changes take place in the current Statistics Canada annual survey of incomes, from which poverty calculations are made:

  (i) that natives living on reserves not be excluded from the survey;

 (ii) that specific information on persons with disabilities be collected following consultation with organizations of these persons;

(iii) that the delay in the release of the annual survey data be reduced to one year.

Appendix A
Social Planning Council of Metropolitan Toronto Budget Outline

A) FOOD - based on standards recommended by the Canadian Council of Nutrition. Basic, healthy food elements.

B) CLOTHING - based partially on recorded low-income household expenditures, plus community panel judgements. Translation of clothing needs into specific items and costs is done by department store purchasing agents.

C) RENT - average rent prevailing for a specified unit in Toronto that year.

D) HOME FURNISHINGS - based on previous budget studies done in other areas, on actual recorded expenditures by low-income families and on the judgements of a community panel.

E) HOUSEHOLD OPERATIONS - calculated in the same way as home furnishings.

F) HEALTH CARE - based on the prevailing cost of various health insurance policies, dental care and drugs, cost of prescription lenses, and basic medicine chest supplies.

G) PERSONAL CARE - based on recorded expenditures by low-income families and the judgement of a community panel.

H) RECREATION, READING, COMMUNICATION - assumes public library availability and inexpensive recreational outlet such as YM/YWCA. Biggest item is a one-week vacation at a nearby rented cottage.

I) ALCOHOL AND TOBACCO - based on data from consumer expenditure surveys.

J) TRANSPORTATION - assumes complete reliance on public transit.

Appendix B
Task Force Budget — National Cost of Living Comparison

I T E M	ST. JOHN'S NFLD.	CHARLOTTETOWN PEI.	GLACE BAY N.S.	ST. JOHN N.B.	MONTREAL QUE.	KINGSTON ONT.	OTTAWA ONT.	SASKATOON SASK.	CALGARY ALTA.	VANCOUVER B.C.
FOOD:										
1. Milk	1.23	0.80	0.94	0.93	0.77	1.09	1.09	0.83	0.81	1.02
2. Cheese	1.97	1.74	1.97	1.89	1.90	1.95	1.69	1.95	1.95	1.89
3. Eggs	1.63	1.55	1.45	1.49	1.50	1.43	1.38	1.38	1.39	1.53
4. Chicken	3.67	3.29	2.84	3.28	4.30	3.29	3.73	3.99	3.95	3.68
5. Ground Beef	3.92	4.39	3.94	2.32	5.03	5.27	3.48	3.29	2.16	3.29
6. Weiners	1.67	1.69	0.89	1.79	2.89	2.13	1.79	1.79	2.89	1.79
7. Orange Juice	2.29	1.85	1.19	1.85	0.85	1.72	1.49	1.89	1.99	1.59
8. Coffee	6.49	5.88	5.99	5.79	7.07	6.85	4.97	5.88	6.39	5.59
9. Tea	2.49	2.09	2.28	1.89	2.36	2.77	2.19	2.49	2.37	2.35
10. Butter	3.09	2.15	2.35	2.33	2.54	2.49	2.29	2.28	2.33	2.41
11. Sugar	1.64	1.39	1.59	1.46	1.83	1.99	1.89	1.74	1.73	1.61
12. Flour	1.98	2.99	3.14	2.89	4.32	2.87	2.69	2.99	3.19	2.75
13. Peanut Butter	2.45	2.19	2.09	2.49	2.36	2.57	1.85	1.88	2.29	2.25
14. Canned Beans	0.99	0.89	0.83	0.79	1.08	1.05	0.79	0.74	0.66	0.97
15. Bananas	1.30	1.21	1.08	0.99	0.64	1.23	0.99	1.24	0.86	1.30
16. Potatoes	3.29	2.59	1.99	2.89	2.29	2.92	2.98	2.39	2.45	2.59
17. Carrots	1.19	0.89	0.79	1.19	0.89	0.99	0.95	0.89	1.35	1.39
18. Bread	1.03	0.98	0.89	0.63	1.07	0.94	1.02	1.09	0.81	1.09
19. Corn Flakes	2.29	1.59	2.16	1.89	2.09	2.26	1.49	1.58	2.19	2.19
20. Jelly Powder	0.55	0.55	0.33	0.29	0.61	0.55	0.44	0.44	0.53	0.55
TOTAL:	$45.16	$40.70	$38.73	$39.07	$46.39	$46.36	$39.19	$40.75	$42.29	$41.83
HOUSEHOLD SUPPLIES:										
1. Detergent	4.18	5.09	2.45	4.99	5.35	5.39	3.49	5.99	5.39	5.75
2. Bathroom Tissue	1.39	2.27	0.99	1.99	1.95	2.24	2.19	2.29	1.44	1.89
3. Scouring Pads	0.46	0.63	0.48	0.29	0.37	0.54	0.40	0.42	0.43	0.38
4. Plastic Wrap	2.25	1.14	1.09	1.09	2.21	2.19	1.99	1.15	1.15	1.17
5. Light Bulbs	2.55	1.01	1.09	1.69	1.62	2.01	2.05	1.69	1.99	1.99
TOTAL:	$10.83	$10.14	$6.10	$10.05	$11.50	$12.37	$10.12	$11.54	$10.40	$11.18
PERSONAL CARE SUPPLIES:										
1. Toothpaste	2.09	1.69	1.99	1.69	1.79	1.92	0.99	2.09	0.99	1.78
2. Facial Tissue	1.35	1.25	1.09	1.29	1.23	1.34	0.89	1.33	0.98	1.35
3. Soap	0.54	0.34	0.33	0.60	0.21	0.40	0.36	0.37	0.36	0.37
4. Razor Blades	2.39	2.49	1.29	1.89	2.39	2.24	1.99	2.49	2.35	2.08
TOTAL:	$6.37	$5.77	$4.70	$5.47	$5.62	$5.90	$4.23	$6.28	$4.68	$5.58

CONTINUED

TASK FORCE BUDGET – NATIONAL COST OF LIVING COMPARISON
REGIONAL COSTS

I T E M	ST. JOHN'S NFLD.	CHARLOTTETOWN PEI.	GLACE BAY N.S.	ST. JOHN N.B.	MONTREAL QUE.	KINGSTON ONT.	OTTAWA ONT.	SASKATOON SASK.	CALGARY ALTA.	VANCOUVER B.C.
HOME FURNISHINGS:										
1. Bed Chesterfield	569.00	399.98	399.98	699.98	599.98	449.49	499.98	499.00	450.00	449.98
2. Mattress & Box Spring	424.00	579.96	419.00	619.96	519.96	434.99	619.96	580.00	620.00	629.86
3. Ironing Board	21.86	17.99	17.99	17.99	17.99	17.98	29.98	26.98	19.99	18.99
4. Electric Kettle	29.99	19.99	24.99	19.99	19.99	26.97	24.99	32.00	29.98	21.99
5. Tea Pot	21.88	27.50	17.95	25.78	25.99	20.25	9.96	6.69	26.69	19.98
TOTAL:	$1066.73	$1045.42	$879.91	$1383.70	$1183.91	$949.68	$1184.87	$1144.67	$1146.66	$1140.90
ALCOHOL & TOBACCO:										
1. Beer	25.54	18.45	17.50	19.00	15.90	15.85	15.85	17.75	17.80	18.20
2. Cigarettes	21.27	14.25	11.89	17.27	13.79	14.74	15.40	13.49	11.29	13.69
TOTAL:	$46.81	$32.70	$29.39	$36.27	$29.69	$30.59	$31.25	$31.24	$29.09	$31.89
READING, RECREATION, EDUCATION:										
1. Newspaper	7.00	6.50	7.00	25.12	18.40	9.25	6.00	7.00	6.75	6.50
2. Telephone	13.15	12.50	12.35	11.75	12.00	9.68	10.50	8.30	7.75	13.20
3. Television	109.00	134.98	122.00	124.98	125.00	103.47	129.98	129.00	99.00	134.98
4. Movie: Adult	4.25	4.25	4.25	4.50	5.00	4.75	4.50	4.50	5.00	5.00
: Child	2.50	2.50	2.50	2.50	2.50	2.00	2.50	2.00	2.50	1.75
TOTAL:	$135.90	$160.73	$148.10	$168.85	$162.90	$129.15	$153.48	$150.80	$121.00	$161.43
MEDICINE CHEST SUPPLIES:										
1. Thermometer	2.59	3.67	2.49	2.99	2.59	2.95	2.09	3.25	2.19	2.48
2. Ointment	4.86	4.39	3.19	5.12	7.60	3.04	4.59	4.50	5.78	4.28
3. Aspirin	2.19	3.29	1.99	1.99	3.33	1.89	2.29	2.59	2.99	1.98
TOTAL:	$9.64	$11.35	$7.67	$10.10	$13.52	$7.88	$8.97	$10.34	$10.96	$8.74

APPENDIX B (continued)

TASK FORCE BUDGET – NATIONAL COST OF LIVING COMPARISON

REGIONAL COSTS

I T E M	ST. JOHN'S NFLD.	CHARLOTTETOWN PEI.	GLACE BAY N.S.	ST. JOHN N.B.	MONTREAL QUE.	KINGSTON ONT.	OTTAWA ONT.	SASKATOON SASK.	CALGARY ALTA.	VANCOUVER B.C.
CLOTHING:										
1. Men's Work Boots	74.99	51.99	51.99	51.99	89.95	49.99	52.99	53.99	69.95	51.99
2. Girl's Running Shoes	26.00	22.99	20.00	12.00	19.99	22.99	13.99	21.98	24.00	19.00
3. Women's Casual Shoes	30.00	20.97	23.00	23.00	14.99	21.95	22.99	20.00	18.95	23.00
4. Boy's Rubber Boots	21.95	10.78	13.00	10.00	9.99	11.99	10.00	9.99	10.00	10.00
5. Jeans	29.98	23.00	29.95	22.00	22.00	18.88	17.00	22.00	26.00	22.00
6. Men's Work Pants	20.00	22.50	17.95	19.00	30.00	12.99	19.99	20.00	21.95	23.00
7. Women's Raincoat	70.00	65.00	65.00	65.00	80.00	80.00	65.00	55.00	49.99	65.00
8. Men's Raincoat	78.88	145.00	145.00	145.00	110.00	145.00	145.00	150.00	150.00	150.00
9. Child's Swampcoat	16.00	16.00	14.95	13.00	9.99	13.88	13.00	17.00	13.00	13.00
10. Briefs	2.69	1.50	2.00	2.25	2.00	1.20	1.99	1.43	1.49	3.00
TOTAL:	$370.49	$379.73	$382.84	$363.24	$388.91	$378.87	$361.95	$371.39	$385.33	$379.99
HOUSING:										
1. Private Sector	520.00	425.00	350.00	275.00	390.00	363.00	441.00	375.00	560.00	572.00
2. Public Housing	269.00	285.00	312.50	301.00	174.35	294.00	294.00	250.00	314.00	345.00
TOTAL:	$789.00	$710.00	$662.50	$576.00	$564.35	$657.00	$735.00	$625.00	$874.00	$917.00
TRANSPORTATION:										
1. Public: Adult	0.60	N/A	0.50	0.75	0.85	0.65	0.85	0.50	1.00	0.85
: Student	0.35	N/A	0.25	0.50	0.25	0.45	0.45	0.35	0.75	0.45
: Child	0.35	N/A	0.25	0.50	0.25	0.45	0.45	0.25	0.75	0.45
2. Monthly Pass: Adult	20.00	N/A	N/A	15.00	24.00	22.00	28.00	18.00	36.00	34.00
: Student	10.00	N/A	N/A	N/A	9.25	15.00	17.50	12.00	7.00	20.00
: Child	10.00	N/A	N/A	N/A	9.25	15.00	17.50	N/A	N/A	20.00
3. Taxi: Flat Rate	1.50	3.00	1.00	2.50	1.20	1.50	1.35	1.40	1.50	1.40
: Additonal/Mile	1.10	0.88	1.00	1.04	1.12	0.50	1.20	1.15	1.00	1.20
4. Gas @ Litre	0.56	0.55	0.55	0.52	0.57	0.44	0.49	0.42	0.41	0.51
TOTAL:	$44.46	***	***	***	$46.74	$55.99	$67.79	***	***	$78.86

*** Because public transit and/or monthly transit passes are not available in these cities, transportation items cannot be totaled.

All items priced are exclusive of provincial sales tax, except the Alcohol and Tobacco items.

An attempt to price the cost-of-living comparison in Winnipeg was unsuccessful.

Appendix C
National Cost of Living Comparison Questionnaire

GENERAL INSTRUCTIONS:

Please read the item descriptions and the pricing instructions carefully. This is necessary in order to ensure that the same items and practices are being employed across the country.

This "shopping list" represents the type of items consumed by a moderate to low-income household. In order to keep the list manageable for this exercise, not all items in a budget are included; this is a sample of items.

The object of this exercise is to compare prices on selected items across the country in order to determine the appropriateness of national standards.

Wherever specified, generally available manufacturers' brands of food items are to be priced. Generic and store brands should be excluded.

Pricing of food, household supplies and personal care products should be done at large supermarket chain stores and/or drugstores, eg. Loblaws, Safeway, etc., in order to provide consistency among the various sites.

The lowest "regular selling price" should be noted.

Clothing and home furnishings should be priced at department stores, family discount clothing stores and/or specialized furniture stores. Please note the name(s) of the stores where pricing is done.

For some items, particularly the home furnishings, it is time-saving to ask a salesperson to indicate the products that fit the sample description.

FOOD:	ITEM	BRAND NAME/COMMENTS	PRICE
1.	MILK	fresh, fluid whole dairy milk, pasteurized; may be homogenized or contain vitamins; disposible carton of 1 litre.	
2.	CHEESE	generally available manufacturers' brands (store brands excluded); process cheese food slices; skim milk powder and/or whey powder added; plain without seasoning or condiments; individually wrapped; 250 grams	
3.	EGGS	large size; grade A; one dozen	
4.	CHICKEN	eviscerated; whole fresh or frozen; broiler, roaster or fryer; 1-2 kg size; grade A; price per kilogram	
5.	GROUND BEEF	medium ground with 24-30% fat content; fresh; price per kilogram	
6.	WIENERS	manufacturers' brands made from beef and pork; ground, skinless, smoked and cooked; vacuum packaged; first grade; 450-454 gram size	
7.	ORANGE JUICE	manufacturers' brands, unsweetened or 5% sugar added; 48 oz. size (1.36 litre)	
8.	COFFEE	Manufacturers' brands; dried instant coffee; pure or may have added dextrin, dextrose or maltose; e.g. Nescafé, Maxwell House. 10 oz (283 grams)	

9. TEA..._____
   Manufacturers' brands; orange pekoe tea bags; package of 60 – 2 cup bags;
   e.g. Red Rose;   8 Oz. (227 grams)

10. BUTTER.._____
    manufacturers or store brand; first grade creamery butter; salted; foil or
    parchment wrapped; 1 pound (454 grams)

11. SUGAR..._____
    white, granulated; cane or beet sugar;   2 kg bag

12. FLOUR..._____
    manufacturers' brands; white, all purpose or bread flour; enriched/vitaminized;
    may be pre-sifted; excluding pastry or other special flours; e.g. Five Roses,
    Robin Hood. 2.5 kilogram bag

13. PEANUT BUTTER..._____
    manufacturers' brands; made from roasted peanuts; may be labelled smooth or
    crunchy; e.g. Kraft.   500 grams

14. BEANS..._____
    manufacturers' brands; cooked beans with pork in tomato sauce; e.g. Libby's
    14 oz. (398 ml) size

15. BANANAS..._____
    first grade; price per kilogram

16. POTATOES.._____
    white, table potatoes; Canada No. 1;   10 pounds (4.54 kg)

17. CARROTS..._____
    tops completely removed; good quality; in plastic or cellophane packages;
    2 pounds (908 grams)

18. BREAD..._____
    manufacturers' brands; pan style standard loaf; sliced and wrapped;
    prepared from white or wheat flour; vitamin enriched;   675 grams

19. CORN FLAKES..._____
    manufacturers' brands; e.g. Kellogs. 675 grams

20. JELLY POWDER.._____
    manufacturers's brands; all purpose, granulated or powdered;   85 grams

HOUSEHOLD SUPPLIES:

1. DETERGENT POWDER..._____
   manufacturers' brands; all purpose granulated or powdered;   6 litres (2.4 kg)

2. BATHROOM TISSUE.._____
   manufacturers' brands; white or pastel shades; medium quality; perforated;
   1-ply sheets, 400 sheets/roll; 4 roll packages

3. SCOURING PADS.._____
   nylon; package of 3

4. PLASTIC WRAP..._____
   manufacturers' brands; 29 cm X 30 m roll

5. LIGHT BULBS.._____
   general utility bulbs; white; 100 watt;   package of 2

PERSONAL CARE SUPPLIES:

1. TOOTHPASTE..._____
   manufacturers' brands; standard dentifrice; may have fluoride;   100 ml

2. FACIAL TISSUE..._____
    manufacturers' brands; 2-ply; <u>package of 200</u> tissues

3. SOAP..._____
    manufacturers' brands of toilet soap; selection confined to wrapped brands
    sold in multiple units of 3 or 4 bars per package; guest or bath sizes, as
    well as varieties with high synthetic or perfume content are excluded;
    e.g. Jergens, Sweetheart; <u>price per bar</u>

4. RAZOR BLADES..._____
    manufacturers' brands; twin-blade cartridges; <u>package of 5</u> blades

<u>CLOTHING</u>:

1. <u>MEN'S WORK BOOTS</u>..._____
    CSA-certified; steel toe and puncture-resistant steel plate midsole; leather
    upper; oil-resistant, non-slip rubber compound sole and heel; 8" high;
    sizes 6-11. e.g. GREB Job-Rated, TUF-MAC

2. GIRL'S RUNNING SHOES.._____
    canvas upper; foam padded; treaded rubber outsole; nylon lined; sizes 1-6.
    e.g. NIKE court shoe, BUSTER BROWN

3. WOMEN'S CASUAL SHOES.._____
    mocassin-style slip-on; man-made upper; nylon-lined; crepe-look sole;
    sizes 5-9. e.g. TENDER TOOTSIES

4. BOY'S RUBBER BOOTS.._____
    "gum-boot" style; fully waterproof; cotton lined; treaded rubber outsole;
    medium width; 12" high; sizes 6-11; black with red sole

5. JEANS.._____
    10 or 14 oz. cotton denim; straight leg western style; 4 or 5 pockets;
    contrasting stitching; boy's sizes 8-16. e.g. LEVI's, GWG

6. MEN'S WORK PANTS..._____
    polyester/cotton; perma-press; scotchguard treated; 4 or 5 pockets; waist
    sizes 30-44, inseam 29-33" e.g. SEARS Wearmaster

7. LADY'S RAINCOAT.._____
    cotton/polyester blend; polyester lining; 2 front pockets; may have detachable
    belt and/or hood; 45" long; Misses sizes 10-18. e.g. CANADIAN MIST II

8. MEN'S RAINCOAT..._____
    poly/cotton trenchcoat with nylon or acetate lining; zip-out insulated liner;
    single-breasted button front; back yoke; belted; sizes 36-46. e.g. RAINTAMER,
    LONDON FOG

9. CHILDREN'S RAINCOAT.._____
    rubber/rayon "swamp coat"; reversible; drawstring hood; concealed metal
    zipper; 2 snap-closure patch pockets; boy's sizes 8-14

10. BRIEFS..._____ /pair
    cotton/polyester blend; elastic waist and leg openings; sani-guard treated;
    sizes 8-14; package of 2 or 3. e.g. JOCKEY, FRUIT-of-the-LOOM

<u>HOUSING</u>:

1. RENT per month in the private sector for an unfurnished
    2-bedroom apartment......................................_____
    - CMHC conducts vacancy surveys each April and October. Suggest contacting
      regional office for information pertaining to your area.
    - Do they include heating & utility costs in the average rental prices given _____

2. RENT per month in public housing for a single working mother earning
    $15,000 per year with two children (girls, aged 4 and 11 years).
    No other special needs..................................._____
    - Suggest contacting the Regional Housing Authority.

HOME FURNISHINGS:

1. BED CHESTERFIELD.._____
   approximately 73" long X 33" wide X 25" high; hardwood/plywood frame;
   no-sag spring back construction; foam-filled reversible seat cushions;
   synthetic fabric; double sized mattress.

2. MATTRESS AND BOX SPRING..._____
   heavy coil construction in box spring; welded grid top and anti-sway
   stabilizers; ½" cotton insulating pad and 1" polyurethane foam padding;
   innerspring mattress; polyester/rayon covering; 10-15 year guarantee;
   e.g. Sears-O-Pedic Regency.

3. IRONING BOARD..._____
   tubular steel construction; mesh top; non-slip feet

4. ELECTRIC KETTLE..._____
   polished stainless steel or chrome-finished; plastic handle and spout;
   automatic shut-off and reset; 2-2 litre capacity; 1500w; e.g. Superior, CGE

5. TEA POT..._____
   pyrex/corning ware; 4-8 cup capacity

RECREATION/READING/COMMUNICATION:

1. NEWSPAPER.._____
   cost of 1 month subscription, delivery 6 days per week; local paper.

2. TELEPHONE.._____
   monthly rental charge for basic black desktop model telephone.

3. TELEVISION..._____
   purchase price of 12" black and white television; AC-DC.

4. MOVIES..._____ A
   admission to theatre showing "family" film (Parental Guidance) for
   Adult, above, and Child (under 12 years).   _____ C

ALCOHOL: BEER: popular, domestic brand; regular strength;
           case of 24 bottles including sales tax   _____

TOBACCO: CIGARETTES: popular brands; kingsize; filter tip;
            carton of 200 including sales tax   _____

TRANSPORTATION:

1. Price per fare of public transit for ADULT: _____
                                        STUDENT: _____
                                        CHILDREN (under 12 years): _____

2. Cost of monthly transit pass (if available) for ADULT: _____
                                                 STUDENT: _____
                                                 CHILD: _____

3. TAXI: basic fare for first _____ kilometer(s)   _____
         for additional kilometers   _____

4. GAS: regular, leaded gas at full-service station;
        price per litre.   _____

MEDICINE CHEST SUPPLIES:

1. Oral thermometer   _____

2. Antiseptic ointment - 60gm tube; for scrapes, cuts, minor burns _____

3. Aspirin - regular strength bottle of 100 tablets   _____

Appendix D
Summary of Family Expenditure, by Size of Area of Residence in Canada, 1978

EXPENDITURE ITEM	AVERAGE DOLLAR EXPENDITURE		RURAL EXPENDITURES AS A % OF URBAN
	URBAN (Pop. 500,000+)	RURAL (Farm/Non-Farm)	
1. Food	3408.9	3010.5	88.3
2. Shelter	3424.3	2414.3	70.5
- rented living quarters	1203.2	237.2	19.7
- owned living quarters	1492.2	1282.9	86.0
- property taxes & assessments	406.3	240.3	59.1
- repairs & maintenance	261.2	324.9	124.4
- mortgage & interest	692.4	581.5	84.0
- water, fuel & electricity	536.1	794.8	148.0
3. Household Operations	814.7	727.2	89.3
- communications	257.9	233.8	90.7
- cleaning supplies	109.7	117.5	107.1
- paper supplies	127.5	124.5	97.6
4. Household Furnishings & Equipment	868.3	837.7	96.5
- furniture	298.4	234.0	78.4
- appliances	168.1	191.2	113.7
5. Clothing	1380.3	1162.8	84.2
- women (14 years+)	678.2	508.7	75.0
- girls (4-13 years)	52.8	71.3	135.0
- men (14 years+)	493.3	416.3	84.4
- boys (4-13 years)	53.8	65.1	121.0
- children (under 4 years)	29.9	38.6	129.1
6. Personal Care	342.7	254.6	74.3
- services (eg. hairstyling, barber)	148.0	86.9	58.7
- toiletries, makeup	150.7	123.9	82.2
7. Medicine & Health Care	400.2	353.7	88.4
- health insurance premiums	151.0	136.9	90.7
- dental care	119.0	82.2	69.1
- physician's care	10.6	5.4	50.9
- hospital care	12.4	10.3	83.1
- prescribed medicine	45.7	57.1	124.9
8. Tobacco & Alcohol	654.3	530.7	81.1
- tobacco products	264.1	235.5	89.2
- beer	152.3	152.5	100.1
- liquor	164.0	117.9	71.9
- wine	73.9	24.9	33.7
9. Transportation	2356.9	2689.0	114.1
- automobile & truck purchase	900.6	1232.1	136.8
- automobile & truck operation	1089.2	1343.2	123.3
- transportation services (local, commuter & intercity)	332.9	103.8	31.2

continued

| EXPENDITURE ITEM | AVERAGE DOLLAR EXPENDITURE | | RURAL EXPENDITURES AS A % OF URBAN |
	URBAN (Pop. 500,000)	RURAL (Farm/Non-Farm)	
10. Recreation, Reading & Education	1244.5	971.8	78.1
- recreation (admission to movies, plays sports events, etc.)	969.3	811.8	83.8
- home recreation equipment	155.9	140.9	90.4
- outdoor recreation equipment	227.0	328.2	144.6
- entertainment appliances	136.3	102.5	75.2
- reading (newspapers, magazines)	122.8	80.4	65.5
- education	152.4	79.6	52.2
- tuition fees	95.6	46.0	48.1
11. Miscellaneous Expenditures	449.1	490.1	109.1
- (eg. interest on personal loans, bank charges, professional & union dues, lawyers' fees, funeral expenses)			
Total Current Consumption (Items 1 - 11 inclusive)	15344.1	13442.3	87.6
12. Personal Taxes, Security & Gifts	5174.5	3331.3	64.3
- personal taxes	3818.5	2314.6	60.6
- security	890.4	599.4	67.3
- life insurance premiums	190.5	149.9	78.7
- retirement & pension fund payments	500.7	313.8	62.7
- gifts & contributions	465.6	417.3	89.6
- religious & charitable organizations	109.7	151.3	137.9
Total Expenditures (Items 1 - 12 inclusive)	20518.6	16773.6	81.7
Income Before Taxes	21505.0	17021.0	79.1
Savings (Income - Expenditures)	986.4	247.4	25.1

Source: Statistics Canada, Family expenditure in Canada, 1978, vol.3.

Appendix E
Distribution of Income, All Families, 1981

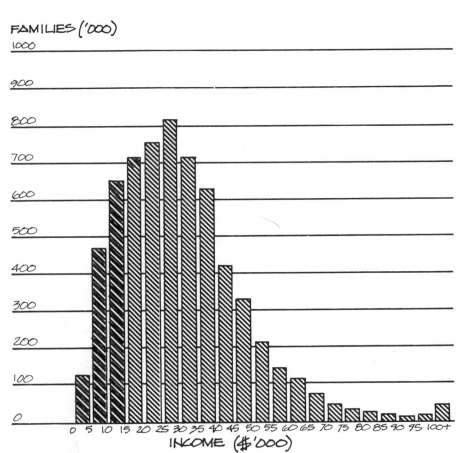

FAMILIES ('000)

INCOME ($'000)

SOURCE: STATISTICS CANADA, <u>INCOME DISTRIBUTIONS BY SIZE IN CANADA,</u>
<u>1981</u> AND UNPUBLISHED DATA FROM THE SURVEY OF CONSUMER
FINANCES, 1982

Appendix F
Distribution of Income, Unattached Individuals, 1981

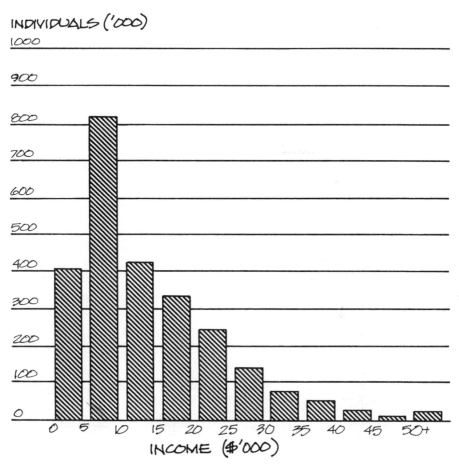

INDIVIDUALS ('000)

INCOME ($'000)

SOURCE: STATISTICS CANADA, INCOME DISTRIBUTIONS BY SIZE IN CANADA, 1981 AND UNPUBLISHED DATA FROM THE SURVEY OF CONSUMER FINANCES, 1982

Appendix G
Distribution of Income, Family Size Three, 1981

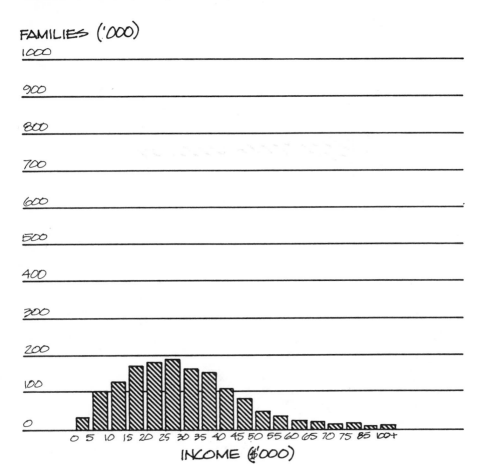

FAMILIES ('000)

INCOME ($'000)

SOURCE: STATISTICS CANADA, <u>INCOME DISTRIBUTIONS BY SIZE IN CANADA,
1981</u> AND UNPUBLISHED DATA FROM THE SURVEY OF CONSUMER
FINANCES, 1982

Appendix H

Percentage of Unattached Individuals by Region, Living Below CCSD Poverty Lines Calculated on the Basis of Average National Family Income, 1981

PERCENTAGE

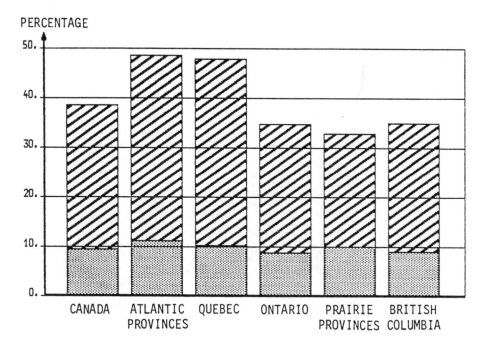

: ANNUAL INCOME BELOW $7610

: ANNUAL INCOME BELOW $3805

Source: Statistics Canada, Income distributions by size in Canada, 1981

85

Appendix I

Percentage of Families, by Region, Living Below CCSD Poverty Lines Calculated on the Basis of Average National Family Income, 1981

PERCENTAGE

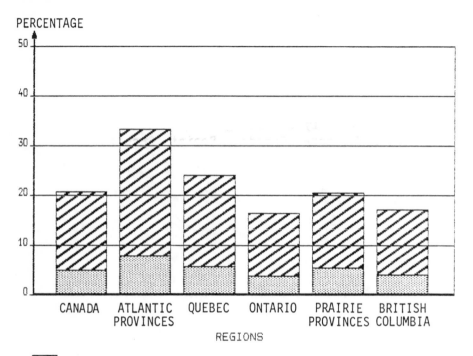

: ANNUAL INCOME BELOW $16001

: ANNUAL INCOME BELOW $8000

Source: Statistics Canada, Income distributions by size in Canada, 1981

Selected Bibliography

Duncan, Greg J. et al, Years of Poverty, Years of Plenty, Institute for Social Research, The University of Michigan, 1984

Health and Welfare Canada, Social Security Research Reports, Research Report No. 01, Characteristics of the Working Poor in Canada, September 1976

National Council of Welfare, 1983 Poverty Lines, Government of Canada Publications, April 1983

National Council of Welfare, Sixty-five and Older, Government of Canada Publications, February 1984

National Council of Welfare, Women and Poverty, Government of Canada Publications, October 1979

Ross, David P., The Canadian Fact Book on Poverty - 1983, James Lorimer & Company Publishers for the Canadian Council on Social Development, 1983

Ryant, Joseph C., Report of the Manitoba Task Force on Social Assistance, Manitoba Task Force on Social Assistance, Winnipeg, September 1983

Social Planning Council of Metropolitan Toronto, Guides for Family Budgeting, 1983, Social Planning Council Publication, 1983

Social Planning Council of Metropolitan Toronto, The Budget Guide Methodology Study, Social Planning Council Publication, 1979

Social Planning Council of Winnipeg, <u>Community Infokit</u>, Social Planning Council of Winnipeg Publication, February 1984

Statistics Canada, <u>Income distributions by size in Canada</u>, catalogue 13-207, Government of Canada Publications

United Way of Lower Mainland, Social Planning and Research, <u>Low Income Basic Family Budgets</u>, March 1982